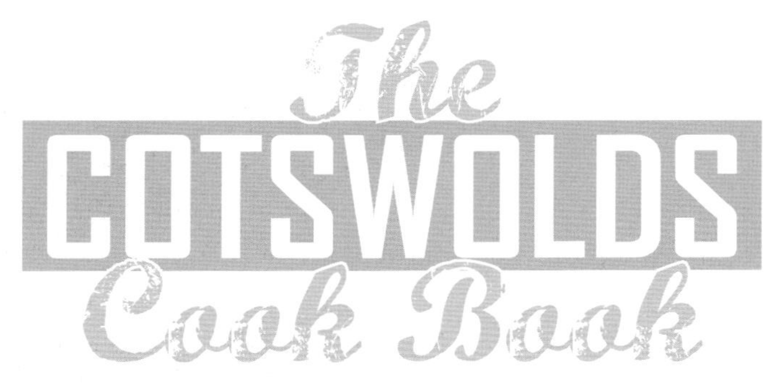

A celebration of the amazing food & drink on our doorstep.
Featuring over 40 stunning recipes.

OCTAVIA'S BOOKSHOP
OCTAVIA'S
BOOKSHOP
ESTABLISHED 2011
OPEN
MONDAY - SATURDAY
9am - 5.30pm
01285 650677
BEER FOR THIRSTY HUMANS
WATER FOR THIRSTY DOGS

Photo: Milosz Maslanka/Shutterstock.com

The Cotswolds Cook Book

First edition printed in 2016 in the UK.

ISBN: 978-1-910863-13-8

Thank you to: David Everitt-Matthias, Le Champignon Sauvage, Cotswold Taste

Compiled by: Anna Tebble

Written by: Kate Reeves-Brown, Rachel Heward

Photography by: Matt Crowder,
Aaron Parsons (www.aaronparsons.co.uk)
Kerry Schofield (www.kerryschofield.co.uk)

Edited by: Phil Turner

Designed by: Matt Crowder, Paul Cocker

PR: Kerre Chen

Cover art: Luke Prest (www.lukeprest.com)

Contributors: Sarah Koriba

Published by Meze Publishing Limited
Unit S8 & S9 Global Works
Penistone Road
Sheffield S6 3AE
Web: www.mezepublishing.co.uk
Tel: 0114 275 7709
Email: info@mezepublishing.co.uk

Printed by Bell & Bain Ltd, Glasgow

FOREWORD

Helen and I opened Le Champignon Sauvage in 1987 when we were won over by the utter charm of The Cotswolds – and thirty years later, I still can't imagine a better place to be a chef.

Although I am a Londoner born and bred, I have now spent more of my life living and working in The Cotswolds than I did in my home city. I learnt my trade in some of London's greatest restaurants, but had always wanted to open my own restaurant with my wife, Helen. When we first saw the premises here we immediately fell in love with the whole area. The laid-back sophistication of Cheltenham was the ideal atmosphere for the type of food we wanted to create.

We love the surroundings. We spend time walking our dog in the beautiful countryside, foraging for food as we go. The Cotswolds are a huge natural larder right on our doorstep. Depending on the season, we can pick wild mushrooms, crab apples, elderflowers and wild leaves, and we are spoilt for choice with the many artisan suppliers in the villages around us.

Using local produce is paramount to letting the seasons influence our menus. Using incredible local suppliers like Cerney Cheese, St Eadburgha Cheese from Broadway, a wonderful rapeseed oil from R-Oil in Stow on the Wold and Sibling Gin in Cheltenham allows us to source not only the finest quality fresh ingredients, but it also means we can get them onto plates in their prime, as well as being able to do so at the fairest prices for our customers.

I am so proud of everything we have achieved at Le Champignon Sauvage over the last 30 years. For me, being awarded two Michelin stars in 2000 was phenomenal, and this accolade cemented into place everything we had been working so hard to achieve. There have been so many highlights for me that it is hard to single them out, but getting the first copy of my first book is a precious memory, as is being awarded an Honorary Doctorate of Philosophy by the University of Gloucestershire in recognition of my culinary achievements and my dedication to championing local, seasonal and foraged produce.

There are so many inspirational places to eat in The Cotswolds – I love The Wild Rabbit Inn in Kingham and 5 North Street in Winchcombe, but there are a plethora of amazing pubs, restaurants, cafés, delis and breweries all around the region, many of which are featured in this book.

I hope you enjoy exploring the food of the region as much as I do.

David Everitt-Matthias

Chef proprietor at Le Champignon Sauvage

Cotswold TASTE

Cotswold Taste was set up in 2016 to promote the incredible food and drink that is produced in the region – and it has become a celebration of the deliciously diverse gastronomic offering here.

Food and drink are an essential part of the Cotswold's offering, alongside a spectacular and distinctive environment, wealth of picturesque villages and historic attractions.

In fact, the unique landscape we call 'the Cotswolds' has been directly shaped by the actions of growing and rearing over many centuries.

"Celebrating and showcasing this precious asset is one aim of Cotswold Taste, the first ever quality marque for food and drink produced to high standards in the region," says Nick Waloff, Executive Chair.

Set up in 2016, Cotswold Taste is emerging as a leading player in promoting the region's exceptional food and drink – and at the same time working to encourage the resilience of the businesses which underpin it.

Some have been in existence for many years and are almost part of the landscape. Others are new, young and vibrant businesses, seeking to explore the edges of taste, flavour and – most importantly, what that elusive word 'local' really means to us. Some are seasonal, and emphasise that they are offering 'one-offs' to be enjoyed for what they are, when they are available.

All of them – farmers, food producers and suppliers, shopkeepers and shop managers, hoteliers, innkeepers, chefs, restaurateurs and the businesses supporting them – have passion as a central element in their motivation, passion to bring you the best. They all have exciting stories to be told.

However, the Cotswolds are facing significant pressures which may affect the environment you see, our lifestyles and even our health. As a result, Cotswold Taste is also an organisation for drawing attention to some of the choices we need to make. There are choices on the part of the food-makers bringing you the recipes and experiences in this cook book, and there are also choices you make as a consumer in terms of what you eat.

"At Cotswold Taste, we believe that quality food and drink can be produced reasonably, and should not be the preserve of just a few. Working together more effectively behind the scenes is one way to keep costs down, and to look at new, more sustainable ways of doing things. This is why Cotswold Taste is a member-owned co-operative, aiming to encourage thought processes, actions and telling the food chain story."

"We also feel that eating and drinking is a conscious act. We need to be more aware of what happens when we ask for, purchase, prepare or consume the food and drink showcased in this Cook Book – both in terms of our own longer term wellbeing and health, and our wider impact on the world around us."

So when you see Cotswold Taste's logo, it means one thing: quality food and drink from the Cotswolds.

Photo: Mark Jarvis Photography

Photo: Mark Jarvis Photography

CONTENTS

Photo: Claudio Divizia/Shutterstock.com

The cider REVOLUTION

Combining tradition with vision… Beard & Sabre are uniting the heritage of ancient British cider-making with contemporary inspiration to put 100% pressed fresh cider in the limelight.

Champions of proper cider, Beard & Sabre is the Gloucestershire-based craft cider company creating artisanal drinks using age-old methods – and they are slowly but surely overthrowing the bland mass-produced corporate offerings with their products.

Beard & Sabre is the brainchild of former Navy officer Tom Dunn, who returned to Cirencester with his cider-making plan after having spent long months dreaming about his venture on board the ship. Craft beer has been so successful over recent years, he wondered why a similar resurgence hadn't occurred in the cider world.

He recruited his friend Angus as director and set about learning everything he could about the art of cider-making – which actually proved to be a difficult task in itself! It was eventually some American producers who were able to shed some light on the secrets of making artisan pressed ciders. They had spotted a niche in the market where traditional cider makers seemed reluctant to tread… adding other ingredients to cider in the way that had been so popular in modern craft beers.

July 2015 saw the business become registered and 35 tonnes of apples arrive on the doorstep – Tom and Angus were not the types to start slowly! The business has evolved and Beard & Sabre has defined for themselves what 'craft' means for them: "At Beard & Sabre we make drinks we ourselves would like to drink, we take our time and we care about the 'small' things, the things that matter. We lovingly craft our cider from the raw ingredients, taking our time in pressing specifically chosen apples in a traditional rack and cloth press."

They don't rehydrate apples and they never water their cider down. They strive to achieve that balance between respecting the heritage of the tradition of cider-making (and doing everything properly) while giving the world some intriguing new tastes to try and pushing the boundaries with some visionary twists. Their first drink was a classic, dry, old-world cider, Apple Smuggler, which was then joined by another four offerings in their revolutionary range – Yardarm, Berrymaster, Blackbeard and Dark Raven.

With their first awards already achieved in 2016, Beard & Sabre plan to continue being a driving force in the cider industry – making sure the art of this British classic drink thrives in the Cotswolds once again.

great taste
2016
Beard And Sabre
Bubbly Shipment
PATT
No.
Beard & Sabre
BERRYMASTER
BLACKBEARD
BLACKBEARD
YARDARM
BERRYMASTER
DARK RAVEN
& Sabre
Cider Co

Beard & Sabre

CIDER AND THYME GLAZED PORK LOIN CHOPS WITH MUSTARD MASH AND RAINBOW CHARD

A quick tasty mid-week supper which looks good enough to serve to guests at the weekend!

Preparation time: 5 minutes | Cooking time: 25 minutes | Serves 4

Ingredients

600g potatoes (Maris Piper or similar)

1 tbsp olive oil

4 pork loin chops

1 jar of Beard & Sabre Cider and Thyme Jelly

Small bunch of thyme, chopped

100g butter

100ml cream

1 tbsp wholegrain mustard

Bunch of rainbow chard, washed and cut up, stalks and leaves

Salt and pepper

Method

Begin by peeling and chopping the potatoes, then boiling them in a pan of salted water until a knife is easily inserted into them. Drain and leave to steam-dry in the pan with the lid on.

Heat a large frying pan up with the olive oil. Season the pork with salt and pepper and a sprinkle of chopped thyme, saving some for garnishing. Cook the chops on each side until golden in colour (4-5 minutes each side), pour over the Cider and Thyme Jelly and cook until the sauce begins to bubble in the pan. Take off the heat and keep warm.

Melt 50g of the butter in heavy-based pan with a lid, add in all of the chard and stir to coat in the butter. Add salt and pepper and fry on high heat for 2-3 minutes. Once sizzling, stir and turn the heat to low, putting the lid on the pan. Shake the pan occasionally.

Mash the potatoes and add some seasoning, the remaining 50g of butter and cream as well as the mustard. Beat well to combine and make smooth.

Divide the mash between four warmed plates, placing it in the middle of each plate. Spoon chard around the outside of the potato and sit one chop on top of each plate of mash. Spoon the glaze over the chop and drizzle it over the chard. Sprinkle with the remaining thyme and enjoy with a glass of Beard & Sabre cider!

Simple PLEASURES

Inspired by her New Zealand roots and grandmother's inscribed recipe books, Jacqui Cowper-Smith continues the family legacy at Beau's Bakehouse in the idyllic village of Frampton-on-Severn.

Jacqui's paternal grandmother Beau's approach to baking has always been the basis for her own business. Running a cake shop with her sisters in New Zealand in the 1930s, everything was simple, but consistently baked to perfection. Many of these tried and tested recipes are still used to this day, though some of the handwritten annotations in Beau's old cook books have needed a fair bit of deciphering!

Taking these traditional methods forward with some of her own creations, it's a combination of a few core ingredients alongside seasonal, natural produce that sets Beau's Bakehouse apart. Free-range eggs and Shipland Mill flour are a must, while figs are made use of in the winter, elderflower in the summer or rhubarb in the spring. And of course Jacqui will always favour butter over margarine; something she was brought up on in New Zealand, it's superior in taste and contains more fat content, preserving the cakes and slices for much longer.

As well as implementing family touches in her cakes and bakes, Jacqui takes inspiration from her collection of over 400 recipe books, gathering ideas and flavour combinations, and adapting with her own little twists.

With just four full time members of staff, plus two in the summer, it's a small operation full of personal touches – for instance everything is hand-packed. The whole model is based upon home baking; not ones to cave to fads or gimmicks (you won't find a cupcake in sight!) everything made here is just a larger scale of what was once created in Jacqui or her grandmother's own kitchen.

With products sold at country fairs, in local cafés, at farm shops, and even events like Jamie Oliver's Big Feastival; it was a deal with Gloucester Services that enabled Beau's Bakehouse to move to a new 900 square foot unit.

"Everybody in the area is hugely supportive of independents; from Holbrook Garage to Primrose Vale farm shop and local post offices – it really is a community effort. Getting Beau's Bakehouse into the services was a huge deal as it meant I could really develop the business. I'm lucky that the staff are just as passionate as I am; they genuinely care about what they do."

With everything made fresh to order, including speciality bakes for those who have intolerances, or are vegan, it seems it won't be long until Jacqui will have to expand her venture even further.

Beau's Bakehouse
Chocolate Brownies
Beau's Bakehouse
Ginger Crunch
Beau's Bakehouse
Chocolate Brownies
Dense brownies made with dark
BEST BEFORE
Beau's Bakehouse
Ginger Crunch
BEST BEFORE

Beau's Bakehouse
ELDERFLOWER AND LEMON CAKE

Inspired by the flowering elderflower hedgerows abundant in the Cotswolds, this cake combines the freshness of lemons with fragrant elderflowers to produce summer in a cake.

Preparation time: 20 minutes | Cooking time: 25 minutes | Serves 10

Ingredients

225g butter, softened

225g caster sugar

4 eggs

225g self-raising flour

40ml elderflower cordial

1 lemon, zest

2 tbsp lemon curd (preferably homemade)

For the drizzle:

60ml elderflower cordial

1 lemon, juice

2 tsp sugar

For the elderflower buttercream:

60g butter, softened

120g icing sugar

2 tbsp elderflower cordial

For the lemon glace icing:

240g icing sugar, sifted

1 lemon, juice and zest

Method

Line the bases of 2 x 8 inch round sponge tins. Preheat the oven to 180°c (170°c fan oven, gas mark 4).

Cream the butter and sugar together for about 5 minutes – it is important that the butter has been softened first.

Gradually beat in the eggs.

Gradually add sifted flour.

Fold in the elderflower cordial and lemon zest.

Spoon into prepared tins and bake for about 20 minutes, until risen and the surface springs back when lightly pressed.

When the sponges come out of the oven, gently heat the drizzle ingredients together until the sugar has dissolved. Spread evenly over both sponges. Leave to cool.

For the elderflower buttercream, cream the butter and icing sugar together until pale and creamy. Add the elderflower cordial and beat until light and fluffy.

To make up, spread one sponge with 2 tablespoons of lemon curd.

Add buttercream to the other sponge and sandwich together.

Make the lemon glace icing by mixing together the sifted icing sugar and lemon juice, adding a little water if necessary to get the right consistency. Drizzle over sponge and top with lemon zest.

Destination DINING

The Bell at Selsley is a village inn where a beautiful backdrop is provided by the Gloucestershire countryside, but where quality cooking has taken centre stage.

A Grade II-listed Cotswolds inn, The Bell Inn boasts a quintessential English charm fitting of its 16th-century heritage. However, thanks to the vision and passion of its owners, it's also a pub that offers something quite unique to its guests.

Mark Payne and his fiancée Sarah bought the pub in July 2015 after they instantly fell in love with it. They had outgrown their successful restaurant Mark@Street in Nailsworth, which they had been running for four years, and the pub simply ticked every box for them. It had been recently renovated in 2013 and they had a vision to build on its refurbishment and to put good food and drink at the heart of the business.

Mark has been cooking since he left school and has cooked in restaurants such as Claridge's in London, where he spent over three years. He and Sarah share a love of food and they have both enjoyed putting their personalities into shaping the food and drink offerings at The Bell Inn.

Pub classics such as burgers, pie and fish and chips are available alongside their creative restaurant menu throughout the day. From the bread to the after-dinner biscuits, everything is made from scratch. They grow an abundance of veg in their allotment and love to serve seasonal meats and local produce.

The pub can now boast listings in The Good Food Guide, The Michelin Guide and The Good Pub Guide, which is an enormous achievement in just 18 months of business. However Sarah and Mark have firmly kept to their belief that it should be a place for the community to come together, as well as a destination for quality dining. A warm welcome (especially from pub dog Bacchus!) always awaits and they encourage "well-behaved children to bring along their parents". They also have the benefit of some lovely rooms for guests to stay the night, too.

Friday fish and chip night is popular, where locals pop by to have a drink and order their takeaway fish and chips. And thanks to Sarah's ever-expanding gin collection (they currently stock a whopping 43 varieties!) they have hosted some hugely enjoyable gin evenings. Gin enthusiast Sarah is the perfect person to talk guests through her collection – and they can even buy a bottle of their favourite to take home, too.

THE BELL
AT SELSLEY

The Bell at Selsley

LOCH DUART SALMON SCOTCH EGG, SMOKED RAREBIT AND PORK AND CIDER RILLETTES

The Scotch eggs are delicious served hot with some toast to mop up the yolk. The rillettes, classic French comfort food with a West Country twist, make a generous 8 portions. The rarebit is delicious on its own or as a late night snack.

Preparation time: 1 hour plus chilling | Cooking time: 4 hours | Serves 6-8

Ingredients

For the Scotch egg:

5 large potatoes (approx. 1.5kg)

7 eggs, boiled for 7 minutes, cooled in iced water and peeled

100g onion, finely diced

300g Loch Duart salmon, diced

40g spinach, finely shredded

Flour, beaten egg and panko breadcrumbs, to coat

Oil, for cooking

Salt and pepper

Celery salt, to serve

For the smoked rarebit:

2 egg yolks

150g Forest Oak smoked cheese from Woefuldane dairy

1 heaped tbsp English mustard

2 tbsp stout or Guinness

2 tsp Worcestershire sauce

4 thick slices sourdough bread

75ml double cream

For the pork and cider rillettes:

1kg pork belly

375ml Beard and Sabre 'Yardarm' cider

3 cloves garlic, peeled

3 bay leaves

2 Granny Smith apples

Salt and pepper

Pork crackling (made from the pork rind) and toast, to serve

Method

For the Scotch egg

Preheat the oven to 180°c. Prick the potatoes and sprinkle with salt. Place on a baking tray and bake for 50 minutes or until cooked. Allow to cool slightly. Cut open and scoop out the cooked flesh (this should yield 900g). Heat a little oil in a pan and sweat the onions down without colouring them. Remove from the heat and allow to cool.

Fluff up the potato flesh with a fork until relatively smooth and then mix in the cooked onions, diced salmon and spinach. Season to taste. Take 170g of the mix and form into a ball. Make a well in the centre, pop the egg into the well and wrap the mixture around it evenly. Roll in seasoned flour, then egg and lastly panko breadcrumbs to give an even coating. Refrigerate for 2 hours.

Preheat the oven to 180°c. Heat the oil for deep-frying to 170°c. Deep-fry the Scotch eggs for 3 minutes then transfer to the oven for a further 3 minutes. Serve hot with a dish of celery salt on the side.

For the smoked rarebit

Place the egg yolk, cheese, mustard, stout and Worcestershire sauce in a food processor and pulse until smooth. Add the cream and carefully pulse until just incorporated. Take care not to overwork and curdle the mixture. Lightly toast the sliced sourdough, spread a generous amount of the cheese mixture on top and grill until golden brown and glazed. Serve immediately. Any leftover mix will keep in the fridge for up to 3 days.

For the pork and cider rillettes

Preheat the oven to 130°c. Remove the rind from the pork belly in one piece (ask your butcher to do this for you) and reserve it to make crackling, which is lovely served with the rillettes. Dice the pork into 5cm dice, place in a heavy casserole dish with the cider, garlic, bay leaves and salt and pepper. Add 1.5 of litres water and bring to the boil. Cover with greaseproof paper and a tight-fitting lid and place in the oven for about 3 hours, until the meat is very soft. If there is any liquid left, bring the mixture back to the boil and reduce slowly until very nearly dry. Drain off and set aside half the fat and remove the bay leaves.

Put the meat into a food mixer and mix with the paddle attachment slowly until it breaks up. Peel and finely dice the apples and mix into the pork. Check the seasoning and add a little of the reserved fat if the mixture is a little dry. Pack the mixture into serving glasses and allow to cool slightly before pouring a little of the remaining fat on top to form a 'cap'. Chill in the refrigerator until cold and set. Serve with homemade pork crackling and some toast.

The Bell at Selsley

GRILLED ROSE VEAL T-BONE WITH CAPONATA SALAD AND SHERRY VINEGAR DRESSING

The light salad and vinegar dressing work so well with the deep, rich flavour of the veal.

Preparation time: 20 minutes | Cooking time: 25 minutes | Serves 4

Ingredients

For the caponata salad:

3 sticks celery, peeled

2 tbsp vegetable oil

1 aubergine, cut into 1cm dice

12 cherry tomatoes, cut in half

1 small shallot, finely sliced

2 tbsp fine capers

2 tbsp roughly chopped green olives

2 tbsp roughly chopped black olives

4 basil leaves, torn

For the steaks and dressing:

4 x 360g Gloucestershire rose veal T-bone steaks (you will probably need to preorder these from you butcher)

50ml sherry vinegar

50ml virgin olive oil

Rocket, celery leaves and parsley, to garnish

Salt and pepper

Method

For the caponata salad

Cut the celery sticks about 5mm thick on a sharp angle. Bring a pan of water to the boil and plunge the celery pieces into the boiling water for 30 seconds until softened very slightly. Remove from the water and drop into ice water to stop them cooking immediately. As soon as the celery is fully cold, remove from the water and turn out onto a kitchen towel to dry.

Heat a large frying pan and add the vegetable oil. As soon as the oil is hot, fry the aubergine, tossing regularly, for 2 minutes until golden brown and softened. Add the cherry tomatoes and sliced shallot and cook for 1 minute, turning regularly. Tip out of the frying pan into a large mixing bowl and allow to cool to room temperature naturally.

Once cool, add all of the other caponata ingredients, mix well and season to taste. Set aside.

For the steaks and dressing

Season the veal chops and either griddle or pan-fry them until medium (approximately 4-5 minutes on either side). Once cooked, transfer all the chops onto one plate and place in a warm area to rest for 5 minutes.

Meanwhile, reduce the sherry vinegar by half in a pan. Remove from the heat. Add the meat juices from the plate with the veal chops resting on (tip away any excess fat first), return the pan to the heat and bring back to the boil. Quickly whisk in the virgin olive oil so that it all emulsifies, season to taste and strain into a serving jug.

To serve

Place each veal chop on a serving plate, split the caponata salad between each plate, garnish with the rocket, celery and parsley leaves. Drizzle with a little of the sherry vinegar dressing and serve.

The Bell at Selsley

BITTER CHOCOLATE FONDANT WITH PISTACHIO ICE CREAM AND CHOCOLATE CRYSTALS

Purely decadent – that's it! The pistachio ice cream is also available to pre-order and buy directly from us at The Bell Inn if you don't have time to make it yourself!

Preparation time: 20 minutes, plus chilling, churning and overnight freezing
Cooking time: 12 minutes | Serves 6

Ingredients

For the fondant:

200g butter

200g 70% dark chocolate, chopped

6 eggs

100g caster sugar

½ tsp table salt

90g plain flour

Icing sugar, to decorate

For the pistachio ice cream:

350ml milk

200ml double cream

1 tbsp glucose syrup

120g pasteurised egg yolk

2 tbsp pistachio compound

100g caster sugar

1 soaked gelatine leaf

For the chocolate crystals:

100g caster sugar

40ml water

40g 70% dark chocolate, roughly chopped

30g pistachio nuts, toasted and chopped

Method

For the fondant:

Gently melt the butter and chocolate in a heatproof bowl over hot water. Do not overheat. Gently whisk the eggs, sugar and salt together until smooth, but do not beat in too much air. Pour the chocolate mixture onto the eggs and fold in until smooth and incorporated. Sift the flour onto the mix and again fold in until all incorporated and smooth.

Line a baking tray with parchment. Grease and line six size-60 rings and place on the lined tray. Pour the mixture into the rings until filled to the brim. Refrigerate for 6 hours.

For the pistachio ice cream:

In a heavy-bottomed saucepan, gently bring the milk, cream and glucose syrup to the boil.

Whisk together the egg yolks, pistachio compound and sugar. Pour the boiling milk over the eggs while continually whisking. Return the mixture to the saucepan and gently heat whilst continually stirring until the mixture coats the back of a wooden spoon. Remove from the heat, stir in the soaked gelatine leaf and then strain into a bowl set over ice. Keep stirring occasionally until cold. Transfer to an ice cream machine and churn according to the manufacturer's instructions. Freeze overnight.

For the chocolate crystals:

Gently melt together the water and sugar occasionally wiping down the sides of the pan with water and a pastry brush to prevent the mixture crystalising too soon. Increase the heat and take it up to 135°c. Remove the pan from the heat and quickly whisk in the chocolate. The mixture will crystalise and take on a sandy texture. Tip out of the pan onto some baking parchment. Allow to cool. Once cool, stir in the pistachio nuts and then place in an airtight container until needed.

To serve:

Preheat a fan oven to 185°c. Place the tray of fondants into the preheated oven and bake for 11-12 minutes. Remove from the oven, allow to stand for 1 minute and then carefully transfer to a serving plate. (Do not remove the ring yet!) Garnish the plate with a sprinkling of the chocolate crystals and a ball of the ice cream. Dust with icing sugar and then carefully remove the ring from the fondant and serve immediately.

A great CATCH

A setting that oozes charm and was once described by William Morris as "the most beautiful village in the England," Bibury is also home to one of the most sustainable trout farms in the country.

Smatterings of ancient and picturesque buildings make up Bibury, with nearby Arlington Mill and Row mentioned in the Doomsday Book, no less. However it's not just the village that draws visitors these days; Bibury Trout Farm prides itself on offering year round supplies of their nationally-recognised brand of trout.

A low-intensity approach, they only allow 10kg per cubic metre, meaning the fish have plenty of room, growing to a healthy size with beautiful fins and tails. Reared in excellent conditions, the freshness is second to none as trout can be taken home on the very same day they are caught.

While the main purpose of the farm is to restock rivers, reservoirs and lakes up and down the UK, it's also an immersive tourist attraction, with visitors coming to enjoy the attractive grounds, feed the fish and even catch their own.

"It's all about the experience of catching it yourself," says owner Kate Marriott. "Some inner city children come and visit, and many have never seen a live fish before. The hunter gatherer aspect is what makes it exciting for them."

If you're more into eating rather than catching fish however, then the café is the best place to sample their wares in the summer. As well as doing all of their own smoking and processing, they freshly make fishcakes, quiches, pâté and much more besides. You can also buy their range of freshly caught fish to take away with you.

A family affair, the farm is ran by husband and wife partnership Kate Marriott and Terry Allen, while Kate's sister Sheena takes care of the retail side of things. Loyal and passionate, most of their other staff have been there just as long as the family, providing unrivalled expertise in the industry.

From supplying local restaurants, markets and wholesalers, to rearing their own eggs (Bibury are one of the few farms that can breed) and smoking fish in their in-house small kiln, the team work hard to ensure Bibury Trout continues its legacy – just look out for their name on the menu the next time you're dining out.

Bibury Trout Farm

Bibury Trout Farm

SMOKED FISHCAKES

These are very popular on our café menu and sell well in the shop and at farmers markets. Simple to make and healthy!

Preparation time: 20 minutes | Cooking time: 45 minutes | Makes 6

Ingredients

8 slices bread

1 large onion

600g Maris Piper potatoes (weight before peeling)

150g hot smoked trout

150g cold smoked trout

Handful flat leaf parsley

Salt and pepper, to season

3 medium sized eggs, beaten

Method

Preheat the oven 180°c.

For the breadcrumbs, grate or add the slices of bread to a food processor until you get evenly sized crumbs. Place on a baking tray and cook for around 15 minutes, or until dry. Set aside to cool. Don't worry if you make too much, they can be kept for up to 10 days in an airtight container.

Dice the onion and sauté in a pan until softened but not brown.

Peel the potatoes and chop into even sized pieces. Boil in salted water until cooked but still firm. Mash when still warm but do not add any butter or milk.

Chop all of the trout and parsley either by hand or in a food processor, but make sure you keep a few larger lumps!

Mix the trout and parsley with the onion and potatoes. This is easier when the potatoes are still warm. Add seasoning but be aware that the smoked fish may be quite salty.

When the mixture is cool, form into six rounded shapes then coat with the beaten egg and then the breadcrumbs.

Line a tray with baking parchment and cook the fishcakes in the preheated oven for 20 minutes or until crisp and golden brown.

Serve warm – they are delicious with mayonnaise or chilli sauce with salad and coleslaw.

Bringing influences from time spent living in continental Europe, Rorie and Ania Scott have created their dream; a modern restaurant combining the best of British and European fare, right in the heart of Stroud.

After living in the French Alps and working as ski instructors for over a decade, Rorie and Ania decided to return to their hometown of Stroud for an entirely new challenge.

Taking over and completely renovating the former Wadworth pub, the renamed Bisley House now offers modern and sleek surroundings to relax in; tiled floors, crisp white walls adorned with contemporary art and a log burning fire make for the perfect casual dining atmosphere.

Inspired by ten years living and traveling in France and Italy, chef patron Rorie favours classic recipes with a twist, combining elements of European gastronomy and beyond, with the finest British (and particularly West Country) produce.

"We like our food to be exciting and reflect the seasonality of British produce, which is why we have a small and regularly changing menu, with a few Bisley House classics, of course. We're constantly experimenting and innovating with what's on offer, what our suppliers have at the time. We'll adapt a dish to include an ingredient that has been brought to us in its prime, which requires agility from both kitchen and front of house staff. It's a rewarding way to work," explains Rorie.

As a free house, they're not restricted to brewery ties, meaning their drinks menu is just as interesting as the food. Their intriguing wine menu, however, is a nod to their European ties. Deciding to buck the trend of offering world wines, Bisley House favour independent Spanish, French, Italian and Portuguese wines to complement their Mediterranean dishes.

After three consecutive years in the Michelin Guide (the only restaurant in Stroud to do so), it's clear the team at Bisley House have created a winning culinary combination.

Bisley House

Bisley House BOUILLABAISSE

The Bouillabaisse is a Marseilles born classic fish dish that can be adapted to use any fish type. We've selected pollock for its sustainability as it's plentiful in British waters. We serve ours with crusty bread and homemade aioli.

Preparation time: 15 minutes | Cooking time: 40 minutes | Serves 4

Ingredients

1 large onion, roughly chopped

1 leek, roughly chopped

1 stick celery, roughly chopped

2 garlic cloves, minced

½ orange, zest

1 star anise

125ml white wine

50ml brandy

2 tbsp tomato purée

500ml fish stock

400g tin chopped tomatoes

Sugar, salt and pepper, to season

1 bulb fennel, cut into 8 wedges, or 8 pieces baby fennel

100ml white wine

Extra virgin olive oil, to drizzle

4 medium sized potatoes, peeled and chopped

4 strands saffron

4 6oz pieces of pollock (one per person)

Fresh parsley, chopped, to garnish

Method

For the bouillabaisse

Sweat the onion, leek and celery off in a pan, adding the garlic at the end once the rest has softened. Flavour with some orange zest and star anise. Now add the white wine, brandy and tomato purée and reduce the liquor down until it becomes sticky. Now add the fish stock and chopped tomatoes. Simmer for 20 minutes, or until the stew thickens nicely. A pinch of sugar helps balance the acidity of the tomatoes. Season with salt and pepper to taste.

For the braised fennel

The beautiful aniseed flavour of fennel complements this fish dish wonderfully, but fennel can be tough if it's not done right. Using baby fennel or fennel wedges, simmer in white wine for 25-30 minutes. When cooked, serve with a drizzle of extra virgin olive oil, sea salt and cracked black pepper.

For the saffron parmentier potatoes

Parmentier means peeled and cubed. Boil the cubed potatoes in salted water with a few strands of saffron until they soften. They will take on a lovely aroma and an irresistible colour. You can finish the potatoes in the oven with some olive oil and salt for a nice bite of texture.

For the fish

You can serve any variety of fish with a bouillabaisse. Marseillaise fishermen would make with stew with any fish from the left over catch. We select pollock because it's a great British sustainable fish that is a delicious alternative to cod.

Oil and season the pollock and fry skin side down in a non-stick frying pan. You can see the fish cooking as its flesh changes colour. Turn halfway through the cooking time (after about 3-4 minutes depending on the size of the piece of fish). The cooked fish should be firm to touch.

To serve

Serve the bouillabaisse in a bowl with the fennel, potatoes and pollock on top so you can see the beautiful colours of the dish, garnishing with freshly chopped parsley.

Wild about local PRODUCE

Chipping Campden is home to the award-winning restaurant The Chef's Dozen, where the passion for seasonal ingredients, game and wild foods is inspired by the incredible local produce all around them.

The 26-seater restaurant, The Chef's Dozen, is renowned for producing some of the best food in the region, but it has also become famous for the way it balances culinary sophistication with a relaxed home-from-home feeling. The husband and wife team behind the award-winning eatery, Richard and Solanche, are as passionate about getting that welcoming ambience just right as they are about showcasing the incredible bounty of produce from the region.

Looking out of the restaurant window, chef Richard Craven can see The Kings Hotel, where he began his career at the age of 15. His journey as a chef has taken him through various kitchens, each of which contributed to his understanding and appreciation of seasonality, provenance and wild foods. Working under the talented Emily Watkins at The Kingham Plough was his first taste of how chefs can respond daily – even hourly – to the produce that is available.

Richard and Solanche spent some time working in South Africa where Richard worked in one of the world's finest restaurants. This period was a huge source of inspiration, particularly the focus on indigenous game, which sparked an interest in the game in the Cotswolds. Wine aficionados will also notice the vineyards of Franschhoek and Stellenbosch are well represented in The Chefs Dozen's wine list.

The aim of the restaurant is simple: for guests to relax and enjoy a leisurely experience, whether they arrive in dinner jackets or wellies. Solanche expertly manages front of house with knowledge about the ever-changing menu, which is adapted depending on what their producers are most excited about. The venison comes from an estate just a mile from the door, cheese from Gorsehill Abbey, pork from Paddock Farm, milk from Cotteswold Dairy, and the game from David Moore family butchers.

The Chef's Dozen allows its location in the Cotswolds to shape its menus, moving with the seasons daily and delighting in the bounty of the natural larder on their doorstep.

the
chef's dozen

The Chef's Dozen

CURED AND POACHED POLLOCK, CUCUMBER, GREEN APPLE AND GENTLEMAN'S RELISH

Almost all of the produce we use at The Chef's Dozen comes from our brilliant Cotswold larder; the majority from within ten miles - with seafood being the obvious exception. As with the rest of our ingredients, we opt for the most sustainable produce available, which usually means anything wild and seasonal. We treat our pollock as simply as possible to allow its flavour to shine.

Preparation time: 15 minutes | Cooking time: 40 minutes | Serves 4

Ingredients

For the sorbet syrup:

750g sugar

650ml water

90g glucose

For the green apple sorbet/granita:

450g green apple purée

150ml sorbet syrup (above)

For the cured pollock:

200g sugar

200g salt

600g fresh pollock (skin off)

For the Gentleman's Relish mayonnaise:

2 egg yolks

1 tbsp French mustard

1 tbsp Gentleman's Relish

½ lemon, juice

200ml rapeseed oil

salt and pepper

For the pollock stock jelly:

500 g pollock bones (any good fishmonger should be able to provide these for you)

100g dried seaweed (try a wholefoods store, otherwise nori sheets from a supermarket would work as an alternative)

1 litre water

Sea salt to taste

6 leaves of gelatine, soaked

Method

For the green apple sorbet/granita

First make the sorbet syrup by heating the sugar, water and glucose to a simmer. Allow to cool. You will need 150ml of the syrup for the sorbet/granita. Purée together the apple purée and the 150ml of syrup and either churn in an ice cream maker for sorbet or set in a tray in the freezer to make granita.

For the cured pollock

Mix the sugar and salt together to create a sweet cure. Liberally cover the fish with the mix, making sure it is completely covered by the sweet cure and leave for 6 hours.

After 6 hours, wash off the cure and pat the fish dry with a paper towel. Split the fish lengthways, separating the belly from the loin and then portion the fish giving approximately 100g per portion, ensuring everyone gets both belly and loin.

For the Gentleman's Relish mayonnaise

Tip everything into a measuring jug. Put a hand blender into the jug so it touches the bottom of the jug, give it a pulse for a few seconds then very gradually pull the blade to the top, and you will have the emulsion ready to put in a squeezy bottle or piping bag for plating.

For the pollock stock jelly

Put the pollock bones and seaweed in a pot with the water and slowly simmer for about an hour (don't boil). The broth will take on a deep umami flavour. We then clarify the stock with an egg raft, before passing through some cheesecloth. (You can just pass it through a fine sieve).

Reduce the stock until you're happy with the flavour and add a little salt to taste. We choose to keep this as 'clean' and as pure a flavour of the pollock as possible. We add 6 leaves of gelatine (softened in water first) to help set the stock into a jelly and then cut into discs for plating for a lovely savoury garnish.

To plate and garnish

Before serving, gently warm the pollock through in simmering water for 3 minutes. Plate the pollock with the sorbet/granita, mayonnaise and jelly. We also use the following, which can be added as you see fit: avruga caviar, cucumber portioned with an extremely small Parisienne scoop, freshly diced Granny Smith apple and salad burnet leaves. Plus we produce a salad brunet oil which has a distinctive cucumber flavour.

In good SPIRITS

The Cotswolds is famous for many things – stunning natural beauty, historic towns and some of the country's finest places to eat and drink. In 2014 it was able to add its own distillery to that list, and the awards are already stacking up...

About five miles south of Shipston-on-Stour are the typical Cotswold villages of Cherington and Stourton, which have become the unlikely setting for a state-of-the-art distillery nestled amidst the rolling Cotswold hills.

The man behind the Cotswolds Distillery, Dan Szor, is a New Yorker who has made this picturesque corner of the Cotswolds his home. He fell in love with the tranquility of the region having spent many holidays in the area, and it was on one of his family weekends here that he was admiring the endless fields of barley growing all around. A dedicated single malt whisky enthusiast, it occurred to him that nobody was distilling it – and he decided there and then that he would be the first to do so!

Dan found the perfect premises in the form of a barn conversion amidst the beautiful countryside that would supply all the ingredients for his drinks, from the barley for whisky to the botanicals for gin. A visit to Scotland resulted in the commission of his very own pair of state-of-the-art Forsyths copper pot stills for the whisky, followed by a trip to Germany to create a bespoke Holstein hybrid still for their Cotswolds Dry Gin.

The first release of Cotswolds Single Malt Whisky is due in October 2017. Much anticipation surrounds its release, especially since the test batch has already been awarded a Liquid Gold Award in Jim Murray's Whisky Bible for the last two years! It's not just the 'not-quite-whisky' that has been accumulating accolades, the gin was awarded 'Best London Dry Gin' in the World Gin Awards 2016, putting the Cotswolds Distillery firmly on the world drinks map.

Dan has put together a close-knit team of whisky and gin enthusiasts who are as passionate about the Cotswolds as they are about their products. They host award-winning tours of the distillery and have quickly established a reputation as one of the most popular attractions in the Cotswolds. The whole team, as well as many of the country's whisky aficionados, are excitedly awaiting the first release of their much anticipated Cotswolds Single Malt Whisky in October 2017... when they will all be raising a glass to the natural bounty of the Cotswolds.

Forsyths
ROTHES
SCOTLAND
SMALL BATCH
TEST BATCH SERIES
COTSWOLDS
DISTILLERY
Single Malt Spirit
Aged 12 months
Natural Colour
Non-chill filtered
100% organic barley
07/10/16
PRODUCT OF ENGLAND
COTSWOLDS
469
2015
SINGLE MALT
678
2016
886
2015
COTSWOLDS
DRY GIN

Cotswolds Distillery

APPLE AND BLACKBERRY CRUMBLE

Forget baking! This delicious dessert cocktail showcases sweet and tart autumn delights with a delicious crumble finish.

Preparation time: 5 minutes | Serves 1

Ingredients

8 blackberries

Ice cubes

45ml Cotswolds Dry Gin

15ml cinnamon liqueur

12.5ml lime juice

50ml apple juice

8ml orgeat (almond syrup)

To decorate:

Oat crumble, for the rim

Apple slices and blackberry

Method

Rim the martini glass with oat crumble.

Muddle the blackberries in a Boston tin, fill with ice and add all the other ingredients.

Shake and strain into a Martini glass.

Decorate with apple slices and a blackberry to serve.

WHISKY SOUR

Silky smooth, with fresh citrus flavours up front and a warming Cotswolds Single Malt Spirit finish.

Preparation time: 5 minutes | Serves 1

Ingredients

60ml Cotswolds Distillery Single Malt Spirit

25ml fresh lemon juice

20ml sugar syrup

2 dashes of angostura bitters

½ egg white

Ice cubes

To decorate:

Lemon wedge and cherry

Method

Dry shake the Cotswolds Distillery Single Malt Spirit, lemon juice, sugar syrup, angostura bitters and egg white.

Add ice to the shaker, shake and fine-strain into a chilled old-fashioned glass.

Decorate with a lemon wedge and cherry and serve.

Striking GOLD

From a university project to a self-sufficient business supplying some of the country's top chefs; Cotswold Gold are leading the way in sustainable and environmentally sound farming, whilst benefitting the culinary community with their unrivalled rapeseed oil products.

It all started when Charlie Bedlam, a third generation farmer and student at Cirencester Agricultural College, was working on a dissertation about adding value to a crop. On the family farm, rapeseed was the only crop not used for other commodities, so, as all good ideas begin, he gathered around the kitchen table and got to work.

Seven years later, the original product of rapeseed oil has grown to include everything from infusions through to mayonnaise, dressings and marinades in sizes from 100ml to 25 litres.

Stocked in local farm shops, delis, garden centres and National Trust venues; it was a conscious decision not to bring Cotswold Gold into mainstream supermarkets, as they wanted to keep its identity and benefits rooted firmly within the local community.

Since its inception the company has always worked with chefs to develop its products, but it was when they appeared on Raymond Blanc's Kitchen Secrets show in 2010 that it really snowballed. They now supply 19 Michelin-starred chefs, amongst hundreds of others across the country. So why do chefs favour Cotswold Gold?

"It has half the saturated fat of olive oil and is high in omega. But the key is that it can reach 240°c without altering the flavour or structure, so it's the best oil to use for frying. Trust us, it makes better roast potatoes than goose fat!" explains Charlie.

"Rapeseed oil is both healthy and versatile, but the best thing about Cotswold Gold is that we grow all the rapeseed on our own farm in the Cotswolds, making the product fully traceable and 100% British," he adds.

They're also extremely environmentally conscious. Once the oil has been used, Cotswold Gold turns the waste into fuel to heat their offices, using a homemade filter system. As a result they are now very close to achieving their zero waste carbon neutral targets.

Though separate, Cotswold Gold relies wholly upon the family farm. Running hand in hand with each other, there's no doubt that Charlie's original aim has been well and truly surpassed.

COTSWOLD GOLD
EXTRA VIRGIN COLD PRESSED RAPESEED OIL
WITH WHITE TRUFFLE
DRIZZLE
COTSWOLD GOLD
Mayonnaise
RICH IN OMEGA 3
COTSWOLD GOLD
Garlic Mayonnaise
RICH IN OMEGA 3

COTSWOLD GOLD

COTSWOLD LIFE
FOOD & DRINK AWARDS
2013 Cotswold Food Hero
Charlie Beldam, Cotswold Gold
Sponsored by

cj HOLE
sales & lettings

BUSINESS
AWARDS 2016
COTSWOLD GOLD

RUSSELL'S

Cotswold Gold

FISH AND CHIPS, MUSHY PEAS AND GARLIC MAYONNAISE

This dish was made by Russell's Fish and Chips of Broadway, who cook everything in my Cotswold Gold Rapeseed Oil.

Preparation time: 15 minutes | Cooking time: 30 minutes | Serves 6

Ingredients

6 sides cod

Flour, for dusting the cod

For the batter:

125g plain flour

120ml milk

120ml water

45g baking powder

1 tsp salt

For the mushy peas:

250g frozen peas

¼ tsp salt

¼ tsp pepper

150ml Cotswold Gold Rapeseed Oil

For the chips:

10 large Maris Piper potatoes

1.5 litres Cotswold Gold Rapeseed Oil

Method

For the batter

Add all of the ingredients together and whisk well. If you would like you can add ale to this – simply substitute 60ml of water for 60ml of ale.

For the mushy peas

Add all of the ingredients to a pan. Bring to the boil, stirring regularly. Cover and simmer for 10 minutes. Crush the peas with a potato masher or electric hand whisk. Add more seasoning to your taste and serve warm.

For the fish and chips

Cut the Maris Pipers into thin or thick chips depending on how you like them. Add to boiling water and leave to soak for 10 minutes. Dry thoroughly on a paper towel.

Add Cotswold Gold Rapeseed Oil to a pan or small deep fryer and heat to 190°c.

Place the cod into the flour on both sides then cover with the batter mix. Add the fish to oil for 4-5 minutes, or until the batter turns golden, then take out and rest. As this rests place the dry chips into to the oil for 4-5 minutes until golden. Take out and leave on a wire rack with a tray underneath to let the residual oil drip off.

To serve

Place all items on a plate and serve with a dollop of Cotswold Gold Garlic Mayonnaise and a slice of lemon.

From a modest egg shed to multiple award-winning farm shop and butchery, Court Farm has come a long way in the last couple of years.

A fourth generation farmer, Simon Knight and his family have been at Court Farm since 1936, producing beef, lamb, Gloucestershire Old Spot pork and free-range eggs. With so much excellent produce on offer, in 2015 Simon and his fiancé Lisa Grayson decided to upgrade their 'egg shed' to a fully functioning farm shop and butchery, and they haven't looked back since.

Lisa explains: "Deciding to diversify and open our own farm shop has been the best decision we have made. Having our own butchery has allowed us to provide our own meat as well as that of local producers, and all to a high standard. All our sausages, burgers and faggots are made in-house and we have over 20 different flavours of sausages as well as a range of meat boxes which our customers love sampling. We also stock a whole host of local produce including bread, dairy, deli and store cupboard items, confectionary, fruit and vegetables, jams and chutneys, ales and ciders, gifts, seasonal plants, compost, garden furniture, logs and local newspapers.

We provide a Christmas meat ordering service throughout November and December when you can order anything from turkeys, geese and three bird roasts, to our famous chicken cushions and gammon or beef joints. The possibilities are endless! A full range of Christmas trees and wreaths are available and you might even get a chance to meet Father Christmas during this festive period!"

It's not just what they sell that has had them receive recognition from local and industry press; as a fully working family farm, the team are keen to introduce people, particularly children, to the lifestyle.

"It's important to teach children about how their food is produced and where it comes from," says Lisa.

Creating an 'animal area' was the first step in achieving this, as well as involvement in a whole host of community events, such as Open Farm Sunday, held annually each June. Activities and demonstrations like sheep shearing, milking and wool spinning involve all of the family, with the most recent event seeing over 2000 visitors descend upon the farm.

Lisa said: "The day was a great success and we look forward to holding the event every year. We feel we have created a fantastic environment to support our own farming practices, as well as other local producers."

COURT
FARM
STOKE ORCHARD
CHELTENHAM
6 FREE RANGE EGGS
CLASS A
6 COURT FARM
FREE RANGE EGGS
CLASS A
www.courtfarmshop.co.uk
Like & Follow Us:
COTSWOLD LIFE
FOOD
& DRINK
AWARDS 2016
Budgens
Best Farm Shop
Court Farm Shop, Cheltenham
Arthur David

Court Farm
LAMB HOTPOT

Simon, a fourth generation farmer on Court Farm, has been producing high quality lamb since he was six years old. He prides himself on providing his livestock with an award-winning level of care and feed. The results of which can be seen in the products prepared in our butchery.

We have been feasting on this hearty, all-in-one lamb hotpot for years and are pleased to be sharing it with you.

Preparation time: 25 minutes | Cooking time: 3 hours | Serves 6

Ingredients

50g Cotswold butter

350g leeks, trimmed and sliced

1 medium onion, chopped

1kg Court Farm lamb shoulder, cubed

Plain flour

1 tbsp Cotswold Gold rapeseed oil

3 garlic cloves, sliced

Sea salt and pepper, to taste

800g potatoes, peeled and sliced

2 tsp fresh parsley, chopped

1 tsp fresh thyme, chopped

400ml lamb stock

120ml Cotteswold Dairy double cream

Method

Melt half the butter in a pan then add the sliced leeks and chopped onion. Stir, and cook over a low heat on the hob for 8-10 minutes, stirring occasionally.

Coat the diced lamb in plain flour (we use Wessex Mill flour for best results).

Remove the leeks and onions from the pan and add the rapeseed oil and garlic cloves. Brown the floured cubes of Court Farm lamb shoulder, adding a pinch of salt and pepper to taste. Once browned, set the lamb and garlic to one side.

Preheat the oven to 170°c.

In a 3.5 litre casserole dish, place a layer of sliced potatoes (approximately half of your prepared potatoes) in the bottom. Season with salt and pepper.

Add the browned cubes of Court Farm lamb and garlic cloves on the layer of potatoes with the cooked leeks and onions on top.

Arrange a layer of overlapping potato slices on top and sprinkle with the chopped fresh parsley and thyme.

Slowly pour in the stock, cover and place the hotpot in the preheated oven. Cook for 1 hour 45 minutes.

Uncover the hotpot and place the rest of the butter on top sporadically. Add the double cream and pop it back in the oven uncovered for 40-45 minutes, until the potatoes are golden brown.

Serve with seasonal vegetables and enjoy!

Court Farm PORCHETTA

Porchetta is a lovely, moist, boneless pork roasting joint of an Italian culinary tradition. Using our own Gloucestershire old spot pork which has been reared on our farm, it is stuffed with a deliciously herby, fruity stuffing and has crisp and crunchy crackling. If you haven't the time to prepare the porchetta joint from scratch, you can buy it fully prepared in our butchery. Just ask a member of our team!

Preparation time: 30 minutes | Cooking time: 2.5 hours | Serves 6

Ingredients

1.5kg Court Farm boneless Gloucestershire old spot pork belly and loin (connected, in one piece)

½ lemon

30g garlic purée

1 tsp fresh sage, chopped

1 tsp fresh oregano, chopped

1 tbsp rapeseed oil

Pinch of sea salt

Fresh seasonal vegetables

Gravy

Method

Pop into Court Farm Shop butchery and ask our butchers to prepare the pork by removing the rind and scoring a diamond pattern. The loin and the belly (in one piece) are then increased in size by cutting and slicing the loin. It should be about half the area bigger afterwards. Our butchers will do this for you if you're not confident enough to try at home.

When you're ready to prepare your porchetta, preheat the oven to 180°c.

Grate and juice half a lemon. Rub the garlic purée on the pork and then sprinkle with lemon zest, lemon juice and freshly chopped sage and oregano.

Roll the pork into a joint.

Place the rind, scored side down on a chopping board. Put the prepared rolled pork on top of the rind and roll the rind around the pork. Trim the excess and tie string around your newly formed porchetta joint. The scored rind should be all the way around on the outside.

Rub the rapeseed oil into the rind and sprinkle a pinch of sea salt over the top.

Put a rack in an oven dish and place the prepared porchetta on top. Put ½ an inch of water in the bottom of the oven dish. Your porchetta should not be touching the water. This will allow the rind to get nice and crispy all the way around.

Cook in the oven for 2½ hours.

The juices from the porchetta will run into the water which you can use as a base for a delicious gravy.

Serve with seasonal vegetables, gravy and apple sauce and enjoy!

Simple FARMING

Traditional sustainable fully integrated farming methods are key at Fir Farm where pasture-fed Hereford cattle are born and raised in the Cotswold countryside.

When it comes to conservation, improving biodiversity and producing top-quality meat, a true passion for sustainable farming is key. When Jane Parker bought Fir Farm she had clear objectives of breeding the finest Herefords, but also of improving the environmental value of the farm. This included increasing bird numbers, improving the River Dikler for wild brown trout and planting an enormous number of trees, thereby providing a habitat for many woodland species and creating a sustainable fuel source for the future.

These pedigree polled Hereford cattle, dating back to 1981, are the pride of the farm, producing breeding bulls and heifers as well as top-quality beef. Herefords, with their distinctive white faces and red coats, are famed for producing quality meat from grass alone which produces excellent marbling and flavour. For Jane and her team, the health of the herd is also paramount and they get the best grass and clover leys to graze on. The herd have accumulated a plethora of awards at various shows and beef tasting competitions thanks to the care and direction of Head Stockman Bob Fletcher.

Firbosa Hereford beef is sold locally within the Cotswolds, but is also available to order directly from the farm through their meat box scheme. The boxes come in a variety of sizes with a mixture of content, such as the BBQ box (which is packed with their famous Firbosa Hereford burgers and steaks), the steak box (which contains rump, fillet, rib eye, braising and sirloin steaks) and different sizes of mixed boxes, which are packed with roasting joints, steaks, brisket and mince.

With free-range eggs, pork, sausages and lamb also available as part of the Fir Farm meat box scheme, the people of the Cotswolds can now enjoy the very best quality sustainable meat, which has been reared right on their doorstep on a traditional family farm.

Firbosa Herefords

Firbosa Herefords

FLAT IRON STEAK WITH GREEN TAHINI AND HORSERADISH SAUCE

A simple way to enjoy Firbosa Hereford flat iron steaks from Fir Farm – the flavour-packed sauce showcases the incredible taste of sustainable grass-fed beef.

Preparation time: 15 minutes | Cooking time: 10 minutes, plus 20 minutes resting | Serves 4

Ingredients

For the steaks:

1kg flat iron steak

Olive oil

Salt and pepper

For the sauce:

2 tbsp roughly chopped dill, tarragon, basil, flat leaf parsley

1 large clove garlic

4cm piece of horseradish, grated

5 tbsp olive oil

2 tbsp light tahini

½ lemon, juiced

1 tbsp white wine vinegar

A pinch of sugar

Method

For the steaks

Season the steak on both sides with salt and pepper, and rub with olive oil. Place a griddle pan (or flat skillet) over a high heat until it is nice and hot. Place the steak in the very hot pan and cook for 3-5 minutes on either side, or until cooked to your liking (3 minutes for rare). Rest the meat for 20 minutes and then slice into 1cm slices to serve.

For the sauce

Place all the ingredients into a food processor and blitz to a smooth paste. It should be the consistency of thick double cream. If it is too thick, add a small amount of water and blend again.

To serve

Divide the rested steak between four plates and serve with the green tahini and horseradish sauce.

A restored fire station provides the perfect setting for a Robata grill to take centre stage – welcome to The Fire Station, where succulent meat is cooked over an open flame and enjoyed in the light and airy spaces of this unique venue.

The Fire Station in Cheltenham was the first time that Mosaic Pub and Dining ventured outside of London and it was the first site they built from scratch. Although the group are experienced restaurateurs, this was an exciting chance for them to really put their passion into action and create a venue that encompasses everything they love about food and drink.

The building itself was a really inspirational prospect for the team. It hadn't been in use for over 10 years, but the original features of the former fire station provided a unique opportunity to create a stunning space. The stair case, the huge doors and the atrium windows were key in developing the bright and spacious feel of the venue. It is perfect for all times of day – sunlight shines through all day long and candles flicker in the evening.

The team drew on inspiration from bars and restaurants around the world while remaining sympathetic to the original features. As they watched the stunning old building come back to life, they were spurred on to make The Fire Station a gorgeous addition to the area and a real hub of the community.

As far as food and drink is concerned, the focus is on simplicity and quality. They have taken great care to make sure the drinks work with the food menu, from beers and wine to those classic cocktails with a twist.

The Robata grill is the centre of the kitchen. Cooking over open flames is ideal in the old fire station, and they have shaped the menu around the grill, allowing it to influence the flavours on offer. Meat and fish take centre stage, complemented by thoughtful sides, however they have been able to accent the menu with creative vegetarian dishes which cook perfectly on the open fire. The menu can be eclectic, influenced by the best dishes from around the world, but using fresh and local produce is paramount.

Still in its early days, The Fire Station is constantly evolving, keeping hold of their key principles but adapting to the desires of their customers and being influenced by the community they have joined.

SNACKS
THE FIRE
STATION
NEGRONI

The Fire Station
BAKED EGGS

A popular light lunch option, our deliciously spiced baked eggs are served with labneh and toasted sourdough.

Preparation time: 5 minutes | Cooking time: 30 minutes | Serves 4

Ingredients

20ml olive oil

2 tbsp harissa paste

2 tsp tomato purée

2 large peppers, cut into 5cm dices

2-3 garlic cloves finally chopped

1 tsp ground cumin

500g tinned tomatoes

8 eggs

8 merguez

4 slices of sourdough, toasted

8 tbsp labneh

Salt and pepper

Coriander cress, to garnish

Method

Heat the oil in a pan over a medium heat, add the harissa, tomato purée, peppers, garlic and cumin, and season with salt and pepper. Allow the peppers to soften, then add the tinned tomatoes. Simmer for 10 minutes and taste for seasoning.

Once sauce has reduced down, add a generous ladle of sauce into a pre heated skillet pan. Make two little dips in the sauce, crack 2 eggs into the dips. Swirl the whites with the sauce, being careful not to break the yolks. Allow the eggs to cook on the top for 2 minutes whilst on the hob, then place the skillet in the oven for 7-8 minutes. The whites should be cooked, the yolks soft.

Grill the two merguez per portion until darkened in colour to a deep rich red, then put them in the oven for 5-6 minutes at 180'c.

Once both parts of the dish are cooked place two merguez on top of the eggs. For serving garnish with a slice of toasted sourdough, two tablespoons of Labneh and coriander cress to finish.

A story in EVERY GLASS

A wine bar and merchant, The Grape Escape mixes all the best bits of a great wine shop with the informality of a modern wine bar to create an inviting haven for wine-lovers in Cheltenham.

The Grape Escape was quick to become a favourite spot for a glass of wine when it opened in May 2015. It is owned by Ant and Zo, whose enthusiasm for great wines was inspired when they worked in London. They watched as the wine scene exploded around them and spent many an evening discussing how much they would love to open their own wine shop in the Cotswolds.

After an inspirational trip to California – which involved lots of vineyards and wine-tasting – Ant and Zo decided that it was time to put their dream into action. They left their jobs, sold their house and moved from Watford to Cheltenham, where they planned to open their wine shop.

The idea was initially for a wine shop where customers could also stay and enjoy a drink, but the idea soon got turned on its head and became a wine bar where people could also buy any of the wines to take home with them. Memories of the trip to California are obvious in the size of the Californian wine section – it's almost as big as the collection from France. For the owners, it's the most exciting region for wine right now and they love to discuss the latest additions with their customers.

They stock 320 wines altogether from 20 different countries, and each week they change the options that are available by the glass so their growing band of regulars always have something new to try. They have a choice of 14 wines served by the glass – usually three sparkling (of which one is English), one rosé, five whites and five reds. Their wine flights have also become really popular too, and they serve cheese, charcuterie, nuts and dips for those essential accompaniments.

Their aim was to create a comfortable and relaxed atmosphere, where fun and friendliness make sure there is no intimidation when it comes to choosing wines. Ant and Zo encourage their customers to try different wines and are happy for people to taste before they buy. More than anything, they want people to enjoy their glass of wine at The Grape Escape as much as they enjoy sourcing it.

The Grape Escape
THE GRAPE ESCAPE
COMA VELLA
Garage
Rock & Roll

Well MATCHED

Ant and Zo from The Grape Escape provide some essential advice on pairing some of our favourite foods with wine...

Here's a top tip – there are actually no rules to food and wine matching. Yes, over the years some partnerships have developed that work particularly well, Muscadet and oysters for example, but the real art of pairing is simply finding wines you enjoy drinking with the dish you are eating.

Lamb

Lamb is such a friendly wine partner. If you're roasting then you can go with the classical options of Rioja or a punchy New World Cabernet Sauvignon. However, this year we've discovered that Carignan and Carmenere both do the trick just as well, if not better! If you're cooking your lamb low and slow you may want to head to the Southern Rhône for a Grenache-heavy Gigonadas or Châteauneuf-du-Pape or, better still, choose north-west Spain and pick up a great bottle from Priorat.

Old World: Priorat
New World: Chilean Carignan

Beef

This may be the easiest meat to match of all – just find yourself a full-bodied red! In Europe we would go for Bordeaux or, for better value, the Syrah-based wines of the Northern Rhône; Crozes Hermitage, St Joseph or Cornas are all great options. Steaks, burgers and barbecued beef were made for New World reds. It could be Malbec from Mendoza or a big, bold Shiraz from the Barossa Valley, but our favourite is a beautiful Zinfandel from Sonoma with a few years of bottle age.

Old World: Cornas
New World: Sonoma Zinfandel

Pork

The first suggestion for pork may come as a surprise but we can't find a better option than an off-dry Riesling.... honestly! The bright citrus fruits, high acidity and slightly sweet finish are a perfect foil for delicious, fatty pork belly or loin with crackling. If you really can't bring yourself to go white then how about a light but bright new world red? Try a Pinot Noir from Mornington Peninsula, or an early-picked Grenache or Zinfandel from California or South Africa.

Old World: Riesling Kabinett
New World: South African Grenache

Poultry

With poultry you can go red or white but make Burgundy your starting point. If red is your thing then go for a good-quality 'Villages' Pinot Noir from Volnay, Aloxe Corton or Nuits St Georges. If you've got a few quid to spend then head straight to Puligny-Montrachet or Meursault for your Chardonnay; if you're looking for something a bit cheaper then St Veran in Mâcon will do just fine. Outside of France we would start our hunt in California, Western Australia or Hemel-en-Aarde at the very tip of South Africa.

Old World: Aloxe Corton
New World: Santa Barbara County Chardonnay

A quick final note about the best match of all... Fish and Chips with English sparkling wine; it really doesn't get any better!

Mas d'en Gil
PRIORAT
COMA VELLA
2010
Garage
WINE CO.
Portezuelo Vineyard
Itata Valley
Carignan field-blend
2013
2015
Chardonnay
CHANIN
2009
Mancini Ranch
Russian River Valley
Zinfandel
Joseph Swan Vineyards
"LA GEYNALE"
Cornas
2009
VINCENT PARIS
VDP
Schloss Johannisberg

Coffee and CREAM

Woefuldane Organic Dairy's popular café and outlet has recently been renamed Henry's Coffee House & Dairy – but the creamy organic dairy produce remains the same, as does Henry's warm welcome.

When it comes to deliciously creamy dairy, the Ravenhill family are experts. The family have been running Woefuldane farm for 12 years having moved to Minchinhampton from the Forest of Dean. Over the years their unique herd of Dairy Shorthorn and Jersey Cross cows have been bred to produce the perfect milk for all of their needs. The farm, which is run by dad Jon, is fully registered organic and the cows can be seen roaming freely on Minchinhampton Common.

Mum Melissa is the cheese-making queen. She's been making cheese for almost 20 years and today the range includes not only cheeses (four hard cheeses, one smoked hard cheese, two blue cheeses, one camembert, up to six variations of fresh cheese!) but butter, milk, cream and yogurt, too. Everything is certified organic and made only with their own milk. Because the milk isn't homogenized, it retains its natural creaminess, and this means that every product is utterly delicious – customers who try their butter are in for a taste of heaven! The cheeses have won countless awards, in fact there isn't a cheese in the range without an accolade to its name.

Son Henry runs the shop and café in the heart of Minchinhampton, where he stocks the full range of the family's produce. The traditional Cotswold building offers a warm welcome to families, holiday-makers, dog-walkers and absolutely everyone else who passes by. The use of reclaimed wood and furniture create a rustic interior, which makes the perfect setting for serving Woefuldane produce alongside plenty of other accompaniments... Think along the lines of local chorizo, interesting crackers, biscuits and handmade chutneys.

The coffee comes from Rave Coffee in Cirencester (with whom they have worked to develop their own blend) and is a coffee-lover's dream when made with their own fresh and creamy milk. Canton leaf teas and artisan cakes from Lavender Bakehouse are also on offer alongside a simple yet tasty savoury menu that exemplifies the quality of the region's produce.

Sandwich of Gloucestershire bacon on homemade bread, perhaps? Or why not sit and enjoy one of Henry's cheeseboards – there is surely no better place than Henry's charming café to sample the award-winning Woefuldane Organic Dairy range.

Perfect CHEESEBOARD

Henry has put together one of his favourite selections of cheeses into the perfect cheeseboard…

Dunlop was our first foray into the world of cheese-making so it's only fair that it sits pretty atop the perfect cheeseboard. It boasts a smooth buttery texture and a flavour that keeps on going with a noticeable bite on the finish. Perfect with a fruity chutney.

Forester is an age-old recipe from the Forest of Dean that was kindly passed down to us by a lady whose family had been making it for generations. Forester is 'old-fashioned' cheese, ripened in cloth. It has a wonderful flavour at any age, maturing to a decent bite and wonderful crumbly texture.

Double Gloucester is a traditional Gloucestershire recipe making it very much at home on our cheeseboard, it has a great traditional texture and complex flavour, which goes extremely well with fresh vine tomatoes and sourdough bread.

Gloucester Rebellion is based on a Single Gloucester recipe. Made from skimmed milk leftover from the butter-making process and matured for 2-3 months, Gloucester Rebellion has a subtle yet memorable flavour which sits very well alongside olives or figs.

Hampton Blue is our own recipe blue cheese, which packs a wonderful Roquefort punch and an extremely rich buttery texture that's somewhere between a hard and soft cheese. Hampton Blue will complement a tasty fruity chutney perfectly or sits well alone on a piece of toasted sourdough bread.

Blue Heaven is our own recipe blue brie. Blue Heaven really is alive! At a young age it has a lovely crumbly texture and soft outer layer, at full maturity it will almost run off the cheeseboard! The Roquefort mould is introduced during the making so it's always there!

What about the chutney? Homemade is always best. Ours is extremely fruity and rich made in batches and allowed to sit for three months while the flavours mingle.

Noel Arms Hotel
PETE BOTT SKIPS Ltd

molemi
The Library
MARK ANNETT
& COMPANY
01386 841622
W424 SDP

Mouthwateringly MEDITERRANEAN

Chipping Camden's high street is home to a little slice of Italy in the form of Huxleys Restaurant and Bar. Set in a stunning 500-year-old house, this is an unexpectedly perfect place to fuse the quintessential English experience with a little Mediterranean passion.

Huxleys Manager Marco fell in love with the Cotswolds having moved to the UK to study English. Today he calls Chipping Camden home where he settled and opened Huxleys. He was born in Bergamo in Northern Italy, and his Italian heritage has been incredibly influential in the development of his business.

"We have worked in restaurants our whole life," Marco and his team explains, "and we just love the way you can make people happy through great food and drink." He opened Huxleys in December 2012 and the café began life serving coffee and cake – and being Italian, Marco certainly knows a thing or two about serving a good cup of coffee!

Marco and his team's ambition for Huxleys was based around its ambience and potential for socialising: "We wanted it to be a place where people could come together. A café to meet, to drink coffee, have a glass of wine and relax. Most importantly we wanted it to feel welcoming for everybody." Huxleys puts a lot of emphasis on the Mediterranean culture of socialising over food and drink, and they encourage customers to take their time and enjoy the company and conversation as much as the dishes.

As time went on, the café grew organically into a small restaurant, to satisfy the high demand of food received from their much-loved regulars. An antipasti selection is perfect for sharing with friends and there are plenty of nibbles on the menu too. Light lunches, salads and fresh fish and meat main courses are also cooked to perfection using top-quality produce in every dish.

They source ingredients locally wherever they can and are lucky to have some great suppliers nearby. However they also import some fabulous Italian produce that they simply cannot find here – or not up to Marco's exacting standards anyway!

When it comes to great ingredients cooked with passion, Huxleys aims to keep a little taste of Italy at the heart of the café – from antipasti and aperitivi to cappuccino and cake.

HUXLEYS
OPEN

Huxleys
PORK AND PEPPERS

This is such a delicious dish and it is simple to make at home. Make sure you use the best pork you can find.

Preparation time: 10 minutes | Cooking time: 30 minutes | Serves 4

Ingredients

4 pork loin

2 large red peppers

2 large yellow peppers

1 large white onion

50g caper berries

1 bag of rocket

Salt and pepper

Olive oil

Method

Preheat the oven to 200°c. Remove the pork loin from the fridge – they need to come to room temperature for 20 minutes before they are cooked.

Roughly chop the peppers and onion. Heat a sauté pan and place the peppers and onion in a drizzle of olive oil and pan-fry until the edges go slightly brown. Transfer to an oven dish and season. Cook for 15-20 minutes in the preheated oven.

Once cooked, add in the caper berries and taste to see if it needs more seasoning.

Heat up a pan large enough to fit all the pork loins, one that you can transfer to the oven if possible. Season and oil the pork, then fry together for 1-2 minutes until you see it caramelize, then turn the pork loins over and repeat for 1-2 minutes. Transfer them to the oven for about 5-6 minutes, until cooked. Allow the pork to rest for about 1 minute.

Arrange the peppers on the plate, dress the rocket with a touch of oil and add to the plate. Slice the pork at an angle and place on top of the peppers. You will find you have a little juice from the rested pork which you can spoon over the pork. Buon Appetito!

Huxleys
SEAFOOD RISOTTO

This is a traditional Italian dish which is a favourite of ours. Use the freshest and best possible ingredients.

Preparation time: 10 minutes | Cooking time: 30 minutes | Serves 4

Ingredients

1 large onion, finely diced

500g risotto rice

150ml white wine

1.5 litres good fish stock, warm

Salt and pepper

1 chilli, diced (or to taste)

2 cloves garlic, diced (or to taste)

500g king prawns

500g squid tubes

500g mussels

Olive oil

Method

Sweat the diced onion in olive oil, without colouring. Once cooked add the rice and a touch more oil to coat the rice, and cook for about 2 minutes. Add the white wine and reduce.

Begin to add warm fish stock, a ladle at a time, while stirring all of the time. It's very important to keep stirring the risotto all the way through the process, as it helps the rice to release the starch contained in the grains, so that you end up with a creamy risotto.

After about 12 minutes of adding stock and stirring the risotto, keep checking the rice to see how firm it is. You are aiming for it to be al dente with a little crunch, but not too much crunch. If it needs more stock add a little at a time. Leave the risotto to the side once cooked.

Heat a sauté pan and add the diced chilli and garlic and straight away add the prawns and squid and fry for about 2-3 minutes, then add the mussels and a touch of wine. Cover so the steam opens the mussels. Any closed mussels must be discarded once you take the lid off.

Place the seafood in the risotto and gently stir, if the risotto is too stiff add a little extra stock and finish with a little butter to make it creamy. Taste for seasoning, then serve straight away. Buon Appetito!

Passion and PRIDE

A 200-year-old butchery business built on a simple philosophy of value, respect and natural farming, Jesse Smith Butchers is synonymous with quality Cotswolds produce.

Getting the finest meats on sale in a butchers shop requires two fundamental elements – farmers who are devoted to rearing high-welfare animals and butchers who have the knowledge, craftsmanship and skill to prepare the meat to perfection. Add a location in one of the country's most beautiful natural landscapes and a heritage that dates back to 1808 and it becomes clear why Jesse Smith is one of the most celebrated meat suppliers in Gloucestershire.

Jesse Smith Butchers is today owned by the Hawes family, who took over the business in 1952. With over 200 years of history, Richard Hawes and his family have kept the traditions of quality butchery at the heart of the business by focusing on provenance, customer service and skillful workmanship. However they have also developed exciting new aspects, meaning that Jesse Smith is no longer renowned just for quality meat, but for a vast selection of delicious produce.

A unique Himalyan salt-lined room is used to dry-age beef to perfection. The pink Himalyan salt bricks draw moisture from the surrounding air and meat, inhibiting the growth of unwanted bacteria. The bricks aid in purifying the air in the chamber and create a sweet, fresh taste in the beef. The butchers is one of only a handful in the UK using this technique.

Alongside beef, pork, lamb, poultry and seasonal game, Jesse Smith is known for the fresh food they make in their kitchen... ready-made meals for a convenient supper, chicken and beef stocks made the traditional way with their own bones, sausage rolls, Scotch eggs, tarts, pastries and not forgetting their famous pies.

In 2016 they proudly opened their farm shop and coffee house in Cirencester, as a celebration of their passion for the area they live in. The family wanted to create a place where the region's amazing produce would be accessible to as many people as possible.

Everything you need to make amazing meals is all under one roof, from their award-winning meat to artisan cakes and breads. The shop contains a deli counter, fresh vegetables, speciality foods from local producers and a relaxing coffee shop where customers can enjoy a freshly made pastry before heading home with their shopping to cook up a taste of the Cotswolds!

Jesse Smith
& W.J. Castle
EST.
1808
Neck
Chuck & Blade
Rib
Sirloin
Rump
Topside & Silverside
Thick Flank
Flank
Brisket
Shin
Shin
Jesse Smith
of the Cotswolds

Jesse Smith Butchers

HOT GAME PIE

This recipe came about due to our insatiable need to use local, fresh and seasonal ingredients to create something to keep you warm in the colder months that's great for all the family. We wanted an outlet to really showcase the wonderful flavour game has, and what better way than with our own pheasants from Cowley shoot.

Preparation time: 30 minutes, plus resting overnight | Cooking time: 45 minutes | Serves 10

Ingredients

For the filling:

500g Jesse Smith pheasant breasts, diced

200g Jesse Smith venison (or venison sausages), diced

300g Jesse Smith smoked streaky bacon (ask our butchers to dice this for you this will save time later, and remember those important bones for your stock)

10 shallots, finely sliced

1 bulb fresh garlic, diced

1 bouquet garni

300g chestnut mushrooms, sliced

1 celeriac, diced into 2cm pieces

150g silver skin onions (optional)

2 litres rich game stock made from the bones if possible (otherwise try our rich chicken stock)

1 tbsp Dijon mustard

2 tbsp red currant jelly

Salt and pepper, to taste

For the pastry:

1kg puff pastry (thawed if frozen)

1 medium egg

Splash of milk

Pinch of salt

To serve:

3 Bramley apples, quartered and cored, then roasted with some Demerara sugar

Method

For the filling

Sear the meats in a hot pan, then remove and set aside for later. Add the shallots and garlic and sauté until caramelised, then add the meats back in followed by the bouquet garni, the mushrooms, celeriac and the silver skin onions if using.

Cover with the stock and add the mustard and the redcurrant jelly. Simmer until the meat is succulent and tender, being careful not to dry out the pheasant or the venison. Once cooked, season with salt and pepper to taste. Cool the mixture overnight.

For the pastry and to serve

The next day, preheat the oven to 180°c. Line the desired pie case with the puff pastry. Fill the pastry case with the pie mixture then top with the remaining pastry. Beat the egg with the milk and the salt and then brush the top of the pie all over to give it a nice glossy glaze.

Cook the pie in the preheated oven for 45-55 minutes or until piping hot in the middle. Serve with the roasted apples. We also like to serve the pie with parsnip and mustard mashed potato and heritage carrots.

Est. 1808

Jesse Smith Butchers
'MR SMITH' BURGER

This is one of our signature burger recipes showcasing not only our prime beef burgers but also our in-house hung beef brisket. We add 'drunk' style onion chutney made with local ale, and top it with our signature cheese sauce, Cotswold cured pancetta and baby gem lettuce. The result is a succulent burger with a depth of 'beefiness' that's second to none.

Preparation time: 30 minutes | Cooking time: 3-4 hours | Serves 4

Ingredients

For our ultimate dry-aged beef brisket:

200g carrots

200g white onions

200g leaks

1 point end dry-aged brisket, cut to approx. 500g

1 bulb smoked garlic

10g crushed black peppercorns

10g salt

1 litre Jesse Smith beef stock

3 bay leaves

30g fresh thyme

20g tomato purée

For the cheese sauce:

60g mature Cheddar cheese

40g Parmesan cheese

300g crème fraîche

2 egg yolks

Salt and pepper

For the 'drunk' style onion jam:

500g red onions, sliced

200g dark brown soft sugar

500ml good quality dark ale

1 bay leaf

1 sprig thyme

A few glugs of Worcestershire sauce

Salt and pepper

For the shoe string onions:

1 onion, thinly sliced

For each burger:

1 x 4oz (115g) Jesse Smith Prime beef burger

1 black onion seeded Brioche bun, fried in our beef dripping

3 slices Cotswold cured pancetta (available in our shops)

3 leaves baby gem lettuce

Method

For our ultimate dry-aged beef brisket

Preheat the oven to 160°c. Prepare all the vegetables by dicing them into 2cm square pieces. Place your boned and rolled brisket in a flameproof pot with a lid and place the remaining ingredients in with it. Cover with the beef stock and bring to the boil. Skim the scum from the top then turn down to a gentle simmer and place a lid on top, then place in the oven for 3-4 hours or until pulling apart.

Take the brisket out of the oven and remove the meat from the juices. Cool the brisket in the fridge then slice thinly ready for later. (Alternatively pop into any of our shops and we would be happy to save you the time.)

For the cheese sauce

Place the first three ingredients in a pan and melt over a gentle heat being careful not to burn.

Take the sauce off the heat and add the yolks, then place back on the heat and whisk until thick and silky smooth. Add the seasoning and you're ready to go.

For the 'drunk' style onion jam

Start by sweating the onions down in a large pan. Once soft and starting to caramelise, add the ale and then the rest of the ingredients. Simmer until jammy, then season to taste.

For the shoe string onions

Deep-fry the onion slices until crispy but not burnt. (If you don't have a deep-fryer you can just crisp them in a frying pan.)

'MR SMITH' construction time

Start by searing your Jesse Smith prime beef burger in a little oil; about 3 minutes on each side depending on how you like your burgers cooked (we like ours a little rare to keep it moist throughout). Slice the bun in half and sear it in the beef dripping cut-side down, until golden and crispy on the cut side only. Finally, sear the pancetta and sliced brisket.

Place the 'drunk' style onion jam on the bun base, followed by two slices of braised brisket and the burger patty. Top with the cheese sauce, pancetta and shoestring onions. Finish it off with a few leaves of crisp baby gem lettuce and then the top of the bun. And BOOM there you have it, our 'MR SMITH' burger.

Jesse Smith Butchers

DRY-AGED TOMAHAWK STEAK SERVED WITH BEEF DRIPPING CHIPS AND BÉARNAISE SAUCE

This is the result of natural farming coupled with expert butchery and maturation. This is the beef 'that built our name'. We like to dry-age our steaks in a purpose-built salt chamber for at least 32 days. This breaks down the fibres in the beef and concentrates the flavour, creating a steak that is deep in flavour and body, as well as tender and succulent.

Preparation time: 1 hour | Cooking time: 20 minutes | Serves 2

Ingredients

For the chips:

3 large potatoes, peeled and cut into thick-cut chips

1kg beef dripping (if not available use vegetable oil)

Salt

For the béarnaise sauce:

1 egg yolk

1 tsp white wine vinegar

100g butter, melted

1 shallot, finely diced

1 sprig tarragon, chopped

For the steak:

1 x 16oz (450g) Jesse Smith dry-aged Hereford, Angus or Longhorn Tomahawk steak

50g butter

1 sprig thyme

Salt and pepper

Method

For the chips

Start by parboiling the chips in salted water (approx. 10 minutes), being careful not to overcook them or they will fall apart. Once boiled, cool the chips in a freezer, then blanch the chips in beef dripping in a deep-fryer at 140°c for approx. 10 minutes. Turn the fryer up to 180°c for later.

For the béarnaise sauce

Prepare a bain-marie. Whisk the egg yolk and vinegar until light and airy in a heatproof bowl, then slowly pour the melted butter onto the yolks and place the bowl over the bain-marie and keep whisking until thickened slightly like mayonnaise. Add the shallot and tarragon then set aside.

For the steak

Preheat the oven to 180°c. Season the steak on both sides with coarse salt and cracked black pepper. Make sure the pan is smoking hot before you add the steak. Once hot, place the steak in the pan and sear for 5 minutes, then turn the steak over and repeat the process on the other side. Add the butter and sprig of thyme and baste the steak thoroughly again and again, then place the pan in the oven and cook for a further 5 minutes or so. This steak should now be medium rare. Remove from the oven and rest for a further 5-10 minutes.

To finish and serve

Whilst the steak is resting, fry the chips for approx. 3 minutes or until golden brown. Drain the fat and season with sea salt. Slice the steak and place it on a plate along with the chips and the sauce, and you're ready to be taken to heaven.

A taste of TOKYO

Hand-painted walls, a cosy basement buzz, freshly made sushi and the tastiest ramen, teriyaki, tempura and katsu curries – KIBOUsushi has brought authentic Japanese food to Cheltenham in an intimate Tokyo-style eatery.

For the owner of KIBOUsushi, Emma Graveney, there was really only one thing about the capital she truly missed when she moved from London to Cheltenham in 2009 – the plethora of authentic Japenese restaurants that dot the city.

An experienced restaurateur, having owned a brasserie in Chelsea and a vegetarian restaurant in Brighton, Emma had the experience needed to open a new eatery, however, with no Japanese heritage herself, she knew she had a lot of work to do to create the authentic Japanese dining experience.

Working with her business partner, Emma set about building the perfect team for the job and, as importantly, finding that elusive venue.

Eventually she found what she was looking for – a 24-seater basement coffee shop, the ideal size and shape to be transformed into an intimate dining space. "I wanted people to feel they had been transported into the buzz of Tokyo when they stepped inside," she explained.

She discovered local artist Martyna Sabadasz who agreed to paint the walls with incredible vivid artwork including captivating illustrations of sushi-eating etiquette. The cosy, vibrant ambience is embodied in the team of staff, most of whom have been working there since day one.

With so much effort going into the atmosphere, Emma was never going to settle for anything other than top-quality fare. Building an excellent relationship with local suppliers such as butcher Peter Jeffries in Cheltenham and fish suppliers Kingfisher Brixham was extremely important to Emma for many reasons, not least for the invaluable advice she and her team are given each day about the day's freshest and best seasonal produce available.

KIBOUsushi is also well-renowned for the wide variety of sake and Japanese whiskies available to customers, either through the menu or to take away through the mini off licence, which means customers are able to buy unique bottles of sake (including aged and sparkling sake) rarely available elsewhere in Gloucestershire. The sake is sourced from family-owned sake producer Akashi-Tai, supplied through London-based company Marussia.

Looking to the future, Emma and her business partner Gilly Read have recently launched KIBOUkitchen, a range of delicious homemade Japanese sauces such as gyoza and tempura sauce, so people in Cheltenham can now create a taste of Japan in their own homes, too. Emma says: "We are so encouraged by the success of the sauces and hope that one day we may be able to sell them via one of the larger supermarkets, that would be a dream come true!"

KIBOU
KITCHEN
満足を味わう
"FEED THE SENSES"
TEMPURA SAUCE
sushi
JAPANESE SINGLE MALT WHISKY

KIBOUSushi

HOW TO COOK THE PERFECT GYOZA

Deep-frying is not a method our chefs would recommend for cooking your gyoza. We don't feel that deep-frying truly shows off the delicate flavour of a really well made dumpling, so we would like to share with you our preferred method which we hope you enjoy using.

Preparation time: 5 minutes | Cooking time: 10 minutes | Serves 1

Ingredients

5 frozen gyoza

1 tablespoon vegetable oil

100ml cold water

White cabbage, thinly sliced, to garnish

KIBOUkitchen Gyoza Sauce, to serve

Method

Place the gyoza in a pre-heated frying pan with a teaspoon of vegetable oil. Pan-fry the gyoza, flat-side down, for approx. 3 minutes, until the flat side of the gyoza is lightly browned, then add 100ml cold water to the frying pan and seal the pan immediately with a lid. Continue to fry the gyoza until the water has evaporated; this will take approximately 6-7 minutes. Remove the gyoza and serve with a garnish of thinly sliced, raw white cabbage and KIBOUkitchen Gyoza Sauce.

CRISPIEST PRAWN TEMPURA

This is a KIBOUsushi customer favourite! You can purchase any KIBOUkitchen products from our restaurant in Cheltenham or call us and we can send you what you need.

Preparation time: 15 minutes | Cooking time: 6 minutes | Serves 1

Ingredients

5 large, raw king prawns (nobashi ebi)

Plain flour

500ml Tempura batter

KIBOUkitchen Tempura Flakes

Vegetable oil

KIBOUkitchen Tempura Sauce or KIBOUkitchen Kimchi Mayo, to serve

Method

Half-fill a rectangular plastic bowl with plain flour and another with the prepared tempura batter (you can buy tempura flour from most supermarkets). Cover the base of a large dining plate with KIBOUkitchen crispy tempura flakes. Heat a deep-fryer to 170°c.

Coat each prawn with plain flour, then dip and fully coat with the prepared tempura batter, then immediately dip and coat the prawns thoroughly in KIBOUsushi Tempura Crispy Flakes. Give each prawn a gentle squeeze with your hand to ensure that the flakes have adhered well, then lay the prawns on a kitchen towel to rest until you are ready to fry them.

Gently immerse the prawns into the hot vegetable oil and cook for 5-6 minutes; the prawns will not change colour much, they will remain a fairly light colour even though they are frying away. Remove the prawns and plate up. Serve with a dipping pot of KIBOUkitchen Tempura Sauce or, equally as delicious, some KIBOUkitchen Kimchi Mayo. Congratulations, you have made, and can now enjoy, the best homemade king prawn tempura at home!

MARKET

QUARE

Chalford CHARM

Customers return to Lavender Bakehouse time and time again for an irresistible taste of Costwolds hospitality – along with all those delicious homemade goodies.

Lavender Bakehouse and Coffee Shop is owned by Tina Bowden who built the business from scratch with the help of family and friends. Having worked in the food industry all her life, the overriding passion had always been to open her own coffee shop bistro.

"I used to drive past the shop on my way back from London late on a Friday night and always thought it would make a brilliant coffee shop or bistro," recalls Tina. It was originally the local Cooperative store for the area with its own bakery and dairy – and they still have the outbuilding where the horses were kept and fed. They tried to retain some of its heritage while bringing in some fresh new charm too, including a lovely hand-painted mural by an artist friend.

The canal-side location in Chalford draws in all who pass by, from local dog walkers and cyclists to walking groups who have come to the area to enjoy its beautiful countryside. Tina and the team cook and bake an array of produce to tempt people in, from traditional breakfasts to something a little different like Turkish-style eggs.

They use local produce from small suppliers where possible, such as Godsells cheese, Day's Cottage apple juice and cider, wines from Woodchester Valley Vineyard, flour from Shipton Mill, coffee from Rave in Cirencester, beer from Stroud Brewery and even a lavender marmalade from Selsley Foods. They also use award-winning, locally produced sausages and bacon in their famous breakfasts... in their first year they were voted one of the top-50 breakfast venues by The Independent.

Each day starts long before breakfast, though. At 5am the team begin baking the cakes and patisseries, which have become so renowned they are now supplied to various other businesses too, as well as being sold in the shop. The shop also provides sandwich platters and cakes for private and business functions in the local area.

By lunchtime it is a hive of activity with homemade soups being served, salads on the deli counter and the smell of freshly made savoury tarts wafting from the kitchen.

Later on, the vintage cake stands take centre stage as the traditional afternoon teas are always made into a special event. White table linens, beautiful china and, of course, a mouth-watering selection of miniature sandwiches, savouries, pastries and cakes – a memorable afternoon each and every time.

Lavender Bakehouse
SAUCE
FRYS COCOA
BOVRIL
LION BRAND
EXTENSION LADDERS
YOU'LL FEEL SAFER
BRASSO
POLISH
Reckitt's
BLUE
LAVENDER
LAND ROVER
Phensic
You can rely on
BEECHAM'S POWDERS
for Colds Chills and Influenza
Sunlight Soap
FAIRY CAKES
...fresh everyday
Gluten free
Homemade tarts
VOLCANO KIT
BUILD YOUR OWN VOLCANO KIT
fresh everyday
Caramel
Butterscotch
Honeycomb
LAVENDER BAKEHOUSE & COFFEE SHOP
20

Lavender Bakehouse

ORANGE AND LAVENDER CAKE

The citrus kick of this gluten-free cake comes from both oranges and lemons – you will need two lemons and four oranges altogether, using the zest for the cake and then the juice in the glaze.

Preparation time: 15 minutes | Cooking time: 60 minutes | Serves 12

Ingredients

For the cake:

700g ground almonds

600g caster sugar

6 tsp (90g) gluten-free baking powder

750ml sunflower oil

16 eggs, beaten

2 lemons, zest

4 oranges, zest

4 tsp dried lavender

For the glaze:

2 lemons, juice

4 oranges, juice

200g caster sugar

4 cloves

4 tsp cinnamon

Method

For the cake

Grease and line a 25cm/10inch round cake tin. Preheat the oven to 160°c.

Mix together the ground almonds, sugar and baking powder. Add the oil and eggs at the same time.

Add the zest of the lemons and oranges and the dried lavender. Mix to combine and pour into the prepared tin.

Bake in the preheated oven and bake for an initial 30 minutes, if cakes are browning too much after 30 minutes, turn the temperature down to 140°c and cover the top with foil. Keep checking the cake every 15 minutes until cooked.

For the glaze

Put juice from the lemons and oranges into a heavy-based saucepan and add the sugar, cloves and cinnamon. Leave on a medium heat until the syrup has reduced by half. Pour half over the baked cake and keep the rest for decoration.

Le Champignon Sauvage

CHOCOLATE AND WALNUT OIL GANACHE WITH ROASTED PEARS

Le Champignon Sauvage is situated within the historic spa town of Cheltenham and has been run by David Everitt-Matthias and his wife Helen since 1987, during which time they have amassed a range of accolades including two Michelin stars. This dessert is a rich chocolate treat with a light taste of walnut, and served with pears in different forms.

Preparation time: 2 hours, plus at least 6 hours chilling | Cooking time: 30 minutes | Serves 12

Ingredients

For the ganache:

375g double cream

50g glucose

200g bitter chocolate (64%), melted

200g milk chocolate, melted

3 egg yolks

3g bitter cocoa powder

75g walnut oil

4g salt

For the roasted pears:

400g caster sugar

1 vanilla pod, split

½ lemon, juice

2 strips lemon zest

2 strips orange zest

4 pears, peeled

40g unsalted butter

40g Demerara sugar

For the pear purée:

3 pears

½ lemon, juice

30g unsalted butter

30g caster sugar

To decorate:

4 pears, peeled

12 walnuts, to grate

Method

For the ganache

Place 125g of the double cream into a thick-bottomed saucepan and bring to the boil. Add the glucose and dissolve in the cream. Remove from heat. Mix the melted chocolates together and pour the cream onto them. Mix until smooth. Set aside.

Whisk the yolks until pale and creamy. Add the cocoa powder. Slowly drizzle in the walnut oil, as if making mayonnaise. Fold this into the chocolate and add the salt. Whisk the remaining 250g double cream to the ribbon stage and fold in.

Using cling film, form the ganache into four sausages (32cm long, 3cm diameter) and place in the fridge to set for 6 hours or overnight. Remove from the fridge and trim the ends through the cling film with a knife dipped in hot water. Cut each sausage into three cylinders and remove the cling film.

For the roasted pears

Place the caster sugar, vanilla pod, lemon juice, orange and lemon zest in a large saucepan with 450ml water. Bring to the boil and simmer for 5 minutes. Add the pears, cover with silicon paper and simmer for 15 minutes, until still firm and just cooked. Allow to cool in the syrup.

Preheat the oven to 180°c. Drain the pears (reserving the cooking liquor) and cut in half. Scoop out the core, then cut each half into three wedges. Heat the butter in a large cast-iron frying pan and, when frothing, add the pears and cook in the oven for 2-3 minutes until coloured. Add the sugar and cook until melted. Then add 30ml of the pear cooking liquor and cook for 2-3 minutes, basting every minute with the pan juices until deep golden brown. Remove the pears and keep warm. Place the juices back on the stove and add 30ml more pear cooking liquor. Bring to the boil, remove from the heat and pass through a fine sieve.

For the pear purée

Peel and finely slice the pears, then toss in lemon juice. Heat the butter in a pan, add the pears and sweat for 3 minutes without colour. Add the sugar, 50ml water and a squeeze of lemon juice. Simmer for 5 minutes until the pears collapse and most of the moisture has evaporated. Blend the pears and remaining juices in a liquidizer. Pass through a fine sieve and season.

For the decoration and presentation

Slice the peeled pear into 1mm slices and cut into discs with a 20mm cutter. Place the chocolate ganache on the plate, then the roasted pear at an angle. Dot pear purée around the plate. Arrange the pear discs and grate the walnuts over the plate. Drizzle with the caramelised pear juices.

LE CHAMPIGNON SAUVAGE

Tailor-made TASTES

From weddings and pop up events, to private cooking in your own home or holiday rental; The Little Pickle catering company offer bespoke experiences from two to 150 diners.

After working as chefs for a luxury holiday company overseas in France, Alex and Jessica Edgecombe decided to take a gamble and start doing things for themselves; with their sights set on the Cotswolds as the hub of their brainchild.

With a thriving independent food and drink scene, plus a real thirst for innovative ideas and talented cooking, the Cotswolds came out on top in their research. Being almost equidistant between Alex's home in London and Jess's hometown in the Midlands, they knew they had hit the nail on the head.

Beginning with small bits of private catering in 2014, it didn't take long for word to spread and for trust to be built up among the best suppliers and producers in the region.

Aiming to use as many local and organic ingredients as possible, Alex and Jess work closely with each client to create a menu to their exact specifications, including wine pairing as an option. Whether Indian, Thai, classic French or modern British, The Little Pickle are versatile in their approach to each booking, which can vary from large outdoor barbecues in the summer to formal catering events and intimate dinner parties in people's homes.

"As we're so adaptable, we've garnered a fair few returning customers and regular clients. Often they'll want something completely different to last time, so we're kept on our toes and no one day is the same," explains Jess.

Running alongside this is the business's other strand. Much like the catering side of things, their range of pickled and preserved products was initially a small-scale operation, but due to its popularity they expanded to the masses. Now offering everything from classic smoked onion chutney and pumpkin piccalilli, through to collaborations with The Cotswolds Distillery (check out their pink grapefruit and gin marmalade or whisky BBQ sauce), you'll find their products at food fairs, festivals and various outlets in the region.

Having doubled in size over the past twelve months, with wedding catering booked far in advance and regular pop ups in new and exciting locations, it seems things are only getting bigger for The Little Pickle.

TOMATO & CHILLI JAM
MULLED PLUM CHUTNEY
PEAR & WALNUT CHUTNEY
PUMPKIN PICCALILLI
LITTLE PICKLE

The Little Pickle

GIN & BEETROOT CURED SALMON WITH BEETROOT SLAW AND SALMON CROQUETTES

This lovely dish makes a perfect spring/summer starter. We use the same botanicals in our curing mix, as in the gin making process to give extra depth of flavour to the salmon. Everything can be made in advance and left in the fridge overnight, so it is great for a dinner party.

Preparation time: 30 minutes plus 6 hours curing | Cooking time: 1 hour | Serves 4

Ingredients

For the cured salmon:

100g salt

100g caster sugar

5g juniper berries

5g black peppercorns

5g coriander seeds

1 lemon, zest

1 bay leaf

20g fresh dill

50ml Cotswolds Distillery dry gin

1 whole raw beetroot, grated

400g skinless and boneless salmon

For the salmon croquette:

30g butter

50g plain flour

100ml milk

200g smoked salmon, diced

Salt and pepper, to taste

20g fresh dill, chives and parsley, finely chopped

100g fresh breadcrumbs

1 egg, whisked

Vegetable oil, for frying

For the beetroot slaw:

150g fresh beetroot

1 shallot

20g fresh dill, chives and parsley, finely chopped

1 tsp wholegrain mustard

3 tbsp rapeseed oil

1 tbsp red wine vinegar

1 tsp honey

Salt and pepper

For the horseradish dressing:

150ml natural yoghurt

50g fresh horseradish, grated

Squeeze of lemon juice

Method

For the cured salmon

Combine the salt, sugar, spices, lemon zest, fresh herbs, gin and grated beetroot in a container. Put the salmon fillet in the middle of the mix ensuring the cure is completely covering the fish. Cover and leave to cure in the fridge for at least 6 hours or overnight.

For the salmon croquette

Start by melting the butter in a saucepan, before adding flour to make a paste. Allow the flour to cook out before gradually adding the milk, whisking constantly to avoid lumps. Take the pan off the heat and fold in the smoked salmon, seasoning and chopped fresh herbs. Leave the mix to cool in the fridge slightly before rolling into balls (about golf ball size). Dust each croquette in flour, then dip in whisked egg before coating in the breadcrumbs. Return to the fridge until ready to serve.

For the beetroot slaw

Roast the beetroot in an oven at 180°c for 1 hour. Leave to cool slightly, then peel off the beetroot skins, before slicing into small wedges. Mix together with the finely sliced shallot, chopped herbs, mustard, rapeseed oil, vinegar, honey and season to taste.

For the horseradish dressing

Mix all the ingredients together, season to taste with salt and pepper and refrigerate until ready to plate up.

To serve

Wash the cure off the salmon, pat dry and then slice into portions. Fry the croquettes in a couple of inches of vegetable oil (or deep fryer) until golden brown. Plate alongside the beetroot slaw and some of the horseradish dressing. We like to put a spoonful of our beetroot, horseradish and gin relish on the dish as well as some picked herbs or salad leaves.

Recognised by customers and the Michelin Guide for its exemplary food and friendly service, Made by Bob has been an essential part of Cirencester's food scene since 2009.

Since Bob Parkinson opened his eatery Made by Bob in Cirencester, it has gained a reputation as a Cotswold dining gem. It has always been popular for breakfast and lunch thanks to Bob's inventive cooking using seasonal ingredients. However it has recently undergone a refurbishment to allow the deli to expand into its own space behind the restaurant, as well as create a new bar area.

The friendly service and inviting atmosphere are important to Bob, and he designed the restaurant and bar in a way that allows guests to feel that they are part of the experience by immersing them in the action. Customers can watch chefs cook in the open plan kitchen or the bartenders shaking cocktails behind the bar.

Food by Bob was awarded a Bib Gourmand by Michelin, which reflects the quality of the food on offer here. The menus change daily depending on what is in season and they strive to use the very best local and international ingredients. The restaurant is open for breakfast and lunch, while Bob's Bar is open during the afternoons.

The bar is also open in the evenings on Wednesday, Thursday and Friday which is when Bob's Bites really come into their own. A selection of small plates inspired from around the world are just perfect to accompany cocktails or wine in the laid-back setting. We're talking moreish nibbles such as wasabi peanuts, polenta chips or Valencia almonds right up to stunning small plates such as burrata with basil, olive oil and grilled ciabatta, steak tartare, or warm octopus and potato salad with smoked paprika.

The deli, now located just behind the restaurant, offers a cafe-style menu for people to enjoy inside or take away. They can also fill their baskets with Made by Bob products such as the homemade dressings and chutneys, as well as daily baked breads, cheese, charcuterie and speciality products from around the world.

When he isn't busy in the restaurant, Bob enjoys doing outside catering. He loves to put together bespoke packages for weddings, parties or events around the Cotswolds, just as much as he loves creating innovative dishes for Made by Bob's daily-changing menus.

MADE BY BOB

Made by Bob

TAGLIATA OF BEEF WITH DEEP-FRIED POLENTA, BLACK TRUFFLE AND WILD MUSHROOMS

This is a quick dish that will please everyone... the prep is easy and will allow you to sit down and enjoy dinner with your guests instead of slaving behind the stove. You can add the meat resting juices to the vinaigrette to give it some extra flavour!

Preparation time: 30 minutes | Cooking time: 20 minutes | Serves 2-3

Ingredients

For the polenta:

600ml water

3 tbsp butter

200g polenta

2 handfuls grated Parmesan

Salt and pepper

For the vinaigrette:

1 tsp Dijon mustard

Splash of Chardonnay vinegar

Grated truffle

100ml olive oil

Salt and pepper

For the steak:

1 double Entrecote steak

100g wild mushrooms

2 cloves garlic, chopped

3 tbsp roughly chopped parsley

Squeeze of lemon juice

Olive oil

Unsalted butter

Salt and pepper

To garnish:

Small handful of dressed rocket

Shaved Parmesan

Grated fresh black truffle

Method

For the polenta

Firstly, prepare the polenta. Bring the water to the boil with the butter and seasoning. Add the polenta and whisk until cooked; about 2-3 minutes. Once thickened add the Parmesan and pour into a tray lined with cling film. Refrigerate for a good few hours until firm.

For the vinaigrette

Whisk the Dijon mustard with the Chardonnay vinegar and seasoning. Add the grated truffle and incorporate the olive oil.

For the steak

Brush the steak with olive oil and season with salt and pepper. Chargrill until cooked to your liking, then let it rest on a wire rack for 5 minutes.

Heat a frying pan, add a good splash of olive oil and sauté the wild mushrooms. Season the mushrooms and, when golden, add a good knob of butter and the garlic. Finish with chopped parsley and lemon.

To assemble and garnish

Deep-fry the polenta until crisp and put to one side. Flash the steak and carve on the bias. Assemble the steak and polenta on a wooden board or slate, slightly warmed, and scatter with the dressed rocket, Parmesan and wild mushrooms. Finish with the grated truffle.

Made by Bob

THAI SQUID SALAD WITH SOUR FRUITS, SHALLOTS, CHILLI, MINT AND CORIANDER

This is one of my favourite salads to put on the menu – people actually ask when we are going to put it on next. It's full of texture, freshness and flavour and just draws your taste buds back and forth if you get the balance right! It's all in the dressing, so please follow the tasting notes.

Preparation time: 30 minutes | Cooking time: 3 minutes | Serves 4

Ingredients

For the dressing:

1 clove garlic

2 coriander roots

2 large long red chillies, deseeded and chopped

Pinch of rock salt

1-2 Thai Bird's Eye chillies

40-50ml fish sauce

2-3 limes, juice (depending on quality, you need about double the amount to fish sauce)

2 tbsp white sugar (approx.)

1 clementine, juice

Small pinch of blue tongue powder (Thai chilli powder)

For the squid:

2 squid, prepared

1 stick lemongrass, finely sliced

8 Thai shallots, peeled and sliced

8 physalis, cut into pieces

1 star fruit, sliced

Green mango, sliced

Kaffir lime leaf

For the rice:

1 cup jasmine rice

1 cup water

1 rice cooker

To garnish:

Good handful of picked mint

Good handful of picked coriander

Method

For the dressing

Pound the garlic, coriander root and long red chillies with the salt in a pestle and mortar. Once smooth, add the Bird's Eye chillies and crush. Add the fish sauce and the lime juice. Taste it, you are looking for a balance of hot, salty and then sour. Once you have this balance, add the sugar. The balance must then be hot, salty, sour and then sweet. Add the clementine juice to soften it and the blue tongue powder for a nice smoky flavour.

For the squid

Prepare and slice the squid. Place the shallots, lemon grass, sour fruits and kaffir lime leaf into a metal bowl. Poach the squid in seasoned boiling water, dipping it in and out to keep the squid nice and tender. Once cooked, add it to the bowl and dress with three good tablespoons of the Thai dressing.

For the rice

Wash the rice gently until the water is clear. Pass through a sieve and put into the rice cooker, cover with 1 cup of water and turn on. When cooked, just fluff the rice gently and leave until ready.

You can do this in a pan with the lid on; follow the same procedure but just cook it on low until the water has all gone.

To garnish and serve

Pick the herbs to garnish – you want slightly more mint than coriander. Add to the squid and gently dress. Serve immediately and serve with the rice.

Towering ABOVE

With elaborate architecture and far-reaching, panoramic views across the country, Broadway Tower has always enticed visitors, from locals to overseas tourists. Named after two of its most influential figures, William Morris and Capability Brown, the modern café is now firmly at the heart of this stunning attraction.

Affectionately known as the "highest little castle" in the Cotswolds, the tower's history is anchored in the visionaries that built it and dwelled within its walls. From founders of the arts and crafts movement to the Royal Observer Corps during the Second World War; the tower has played its part in inspiring great British culture, as well as defending the lives of its citizens.

These days, the tower showcases this heritage through its exhibitions, while the Morris & Brown café binds tradition with location through its locally-inspired menu. Dishes like goats cheese and pear salad and the Cotswolds ploughman's lunch are just a couple of examples of how the café makes connections to the local area, evoking the natural beauty of the landscape.

"Our food is simple and straightforward. We focus on the essentials and do it well, using the best locally sourced ingredients where possible," says managing director Annette Gorton.

With a bright and design-led interior, Morris & Brown offers an informal ambience for visitors to relax in, whether they've been hiking in the surrounding countryside (dogs are welcome too!) or are there just to meet up with friends.

The front of house team, centred around restaurant manager Steve Wood, strive to get to know everyone who walks through the doors, offering a warm welcome to regulars and new faces alike.

"Broadway Tower is a point of emotional connection," says Annette. "It holds a place in peoples' hearts and we often get enquires from people requesting to propose to their loved ones at the top of the tower. It has a sentimental pull to daily life."

"A tourist attraction needs to be a two sided sword. To those visiting from abroad it should show the history and heritage, but all of that is superficial if you don't provide a place that matters to the local community too. At Broadway Tower I think we've worked hard to achieve that balance."

Morris & Brown Cafe at Broadway Tower
Menu
MORRIS & BROWN

Morris & Brown Café

GOATS CHEESE, PEAR AND PECAN SALAD

This fresh dish combines our love of Cotswold produce with the rich tradition of fruit and vegetables growing in the Vale of Evesham. The locally made creamy ash-coated goats cheese is combined with pears and caramelised pecans producing a mix of savoury and sweet - ideal for spring or summer.

Preparation time: 20 minutes | Cooking time: 2 hours | Serves 5

Ingredients

For the spiced poached pears:

500ml water

200g brown sugar

1 orange

2 cloves

4 juniper berries

4 black peppercorns

1 cinnamon stick

5 Rocha pears

For the caramelised pecans:

1 egg white

250g pecans

50g soft brown sugar

For the balsamic glaze:

250ml balsamic vinegar

6 sprigs of thyme

10ml lemon juice

For the salad:

150g mixed salad leaves

100g finely sliced fresh pear

150g cherry tomatoes

36 chopped caramelised pecans

250g ash coated goat's cheese (we recommend Carney Ash)

Method

Make the poached pears, caramelised pecans and balsamic glaze in advance.

For the pears, put the water and the sugar in a pan and heat until the sugar is dissolved. Turn the heat down to just below a simmer. Zest and juice the orange and add both to the sugar syrup, along with the cloves, juniper berries, peppercorns and the cinnamon stick. Peel the pears, leaving the stalks on. Add to the syrup and cook on a low heat until slightly translucent for 1 hour. Once cooled, they can be kept in the syrup in the fridge for several days.

For the caramelised pecans, line a baking tray with parchment and preheat the oven to 180°c. Beat the egg white until it forms soft peaks, add the pecans and mix together. Add the sugar and mix again. Spread out onto the lined tray and bake until golden brown. These will store for several weeks if kept in an airtight container.

For the glaze, pour the balsamic vinegar into a saucepan, add the thyme sprigs whole and reduce on a gentle heat until 40% of the original volume. Add lemon juice and allow to cool. Keep in a bottle in the fridge.

To serve, put a small amount of balsamic glaze on the plate add 1 whole poached pear upright. In a bowl mix the salad leaves with the sliced pear and arrange on the plate topped with chopped pecans and halved tomatoes.

Slice the goat's cheese into five pieces, place on a baking tray with greaseproof paper and cook in a preheated oven for about 2 minutes (time will vary depending on the cheese and ripeness) until slightly softened, transfer to the plate and serve immediately.

Playful AUTHENTICITY

From its beautiful location in the heart of Stow-on-the-Wold, The Old Stocks Inn is a 17th-centruy coaching inn where there is always something new to explore.

It was a tired-looking building before it underwent a top-to-toe refurbishment that took over four months to complete. When it reopened in March 2015, The Old Stocks Inn unveiled an innovative blend of modern luxury and stunning 17th-centruy charm. It is managed by Charlotte and Richard Tuck, with the help of puppy Ralph who wins the affections of every guest!

It is a place that doesn't settle for being just one thing. The beautifully restored building houses a light and airy interior that has been created with an Anglo-Scandi approach to décor. On closer inspection you may notice the individuality is thanks to the use of British heritage designers, with all the furniture crafted in the UK.

The ethos and culture extends from the ambience through to the staff, rooms, cocktails, wine and of course the food to come together into a uniquely boutique experience. General Manager Charlotte describes it as "always giving the unexpected," whatever aspect of The Old Stocks Inn the guests wish to explore. They founded the business on the principles of generosity, curiosity, individuality and playful authenticity and these ideas run through everything they do.

Head chef Wayne Sullivan joined the team in May 2016 and his culinary creativity, which was exemplified in his appearance in BBC's MasterChef the Professionals in 2016, embodies all of these principles. His dishes are never over-described so there is always an element of intrigue when it comes to choosing from the menu. This allows the staff to engage with the customers and help them explore the ingredients, tastes and textures on offer.

Generous hospitality is vital for the whole team, which can be seen in the carefully selected ingredients that are used not only in the cooking, but also in the cocktails for which The Old Stocks Inn has become known for. Head bar tender Pete Simpson uses top-quality spirits from small producers and intriguing flavourings for a boutique bar experience.

Beautifully appointed rooms, a glorious three-tiered outdoor terrace for alfresco dining (complete with wood-fired pizza oven in summer) and the adjoining Little Stocks Coffee Shop, serving artisan coffee and tasty bites, complete this uniquely inspired boutique hotel.

IT'S NEVER
TOO EARLY...
O
S
OTHELLO
£50

The Old Stocks Inn

ROASTED DUCK BREAST WITH PICKLED PEACH

"This dish comprises almond quinoa, sweet potato and charred sprouting broccoli. In the restaurant, it is finished with a sumac tuile. This is a dish of mine that has evolved from a very basic concept imagined 4 years ago. I've refined it enough to proudly use as my 'signature dish' on MasterChef The Professionals 2016. It's a delicately balanced dish bringing richness of the duck into play with fresh, zingy peach and earthy nutty quinoa." – Wayne Sullivan, head chef

Preparation time: 35 minutes | Cooking time: 45 minutes | Serves 4

Ingredients

1 whole Creedy Carver duck (3kg)

Smoked Maldon salt

250g purple sprouting broccoli, trimmed

For the quinoa:

Olive oil

100g flaked almonds

250g black quinoa

250ml chicken stock

For the sweet potato:

2 large sweet potato, peeled

100g unsalted butter

200ml whole milk

For the sauce:

1 peach, stoned

2 banana shallots, peeled and sliced

1 clove garlic, peeled and sliced

1 carrot, peeled and sliced

100ml white wine

Star anise

500ml chicken stock

For the peach:

25g brown sugar

25ml sherry wine vinegar

2 peaches, stoned

Method

For the duck and broccoli

Preheat the oven to 180°c. Remove both breasts from the duck, trim, score, season with smoked Maldon salt and set aside. Break down the duck carcass and roast off the bones for sauce. Place the duck breasts in a warm pan, skin-side down, and gently render the fat, while crisping the skin. Increase the heat slightly and remove the fat from the pan occasionally. Seal the flesh side before returning onto the skin and placing in the oven for 6 minutes. Remove from the pan and rest on a cooling rack, skin-side down. Sauté the broccoli in the pan the duck was cooked in, then lightly blowtorch to finish.

For the quinoa

Add a little olive oil to a warm pan and gently warm the almonds until they begin to colour. Remove the almonds. Add the quinoa to the pan and toast until you can smell the grain (a little like popcorn). Add the stock and bring to the boil. Reduce to a simmer, add the almonds back in, cover and cook for 10 minutes. Break down the grain with a fork and finish with seasoning and olive oil.

For the sweet potato

Cut the sweet potato into 1cm dice. Place in a pan with the butter and cover with a lid. When the butter is melted and turning nut brown, add the milk, replace the lid and bring to the boil. Reduce to a simmer for 10 minutes until soft. Remove from the heat, strain through a chinois but retain the liquid. Place the potato in a Thermomix with 50% liquid. Blitz. Check for consistency and seasoning, it should be velvety smooth. Pass through a chinois, and then funnel into a squeezy bottle.

For the sauce

Caramelise the peach, shallots, garlic and carrot in a pan until golden brown. Deglaze with white wine, add the star anise and reduce the wine to virtually nothing. Add the roasted duck bones and chicken stock, bring to the boil, reduce by half and pass through a chinois.

For the peach

Place the sugar and vinegar in a pan and warm to dissolve the sugar. Place the peaches in a vacpac bag with the pickle solution. Vacuum for 30 seconds. Remove the peaches and sear in a pan over a high heat until caramelised.

To serve

Trim the duck breast and arrange everything on the plate as shown. Finish the dish with a sumac tuile.

The Old Stocks Inn

THE NIFTY ITALIAN

Two cocktail recipes from the innovative bar menu at The Old Stocks Inn. Created by head bartender, Pete Simpson.

Preparation time: 5 minutes | Serves 1

Ingredients

15ml sugar syrup or agave syrup

5 basil leaves

15ml lemon juice

25ml Cotswold Dry Gin

25ml Aperol

Prosecco, to top up

Glass:

Rocks glass

Garnish:

Basil leaf

Method

Muddle (with muddler, rolling pin or wooden spoon handle) the sugar syrup, basil leaves and lemon juice together in the base of the glass part of a two-part Boston Shaker or a jam jar until the leaves are slightly bruised.

Then add the gin, Aperol and ice to top of glass.

Shake vigorously with the Boston Shaker until frost appears on the metal Boston Shaker.

Pour all of your ingredients into a rocks glass and top up with prosecco.

Garnish with a whole basil leaf to finish. Enjoy!

BEES MAKE HONEY

Preparation time: 5 minutes | Serves 1

Ingredients

50ml Stolichnaya vodka (or other premium vodka)

100ml apple juice

15ml runny honey (warm your spoon to measure)

Squeeze of fresh lime

Glass:

Rocks glass

Garnish:

Lavender sprig

Method

Add all the ingredients into the glass part of a two-part Boston Shaker and add ice to the top of the glass.

Shake vigorously with the Boston Shaker until frost appears on the metal Boston Shaker.

Then strain into a rocks glass.

Garnish with a lavender sprig. Enjoy!

RY
01285 652947
RESTORATION & CLEANING SERVICES
Handmade bread
for everyone
FARMERS
MARKET

HORTON CHEMIST

Steak and COCKTAILS

Small plates, succulent steaks and creative cocktails are served in the cosy atmosphere of the Georgian townhouse basement – The Ox has found its perfect home in the heart of Cheltenham.

The Ox Cheltenham is the first foray outside of Bristol for the incredibly successful Hyde & Co Leisure, the team behind the small group of relaxed restaurants and speakeasy-style bars. Their love of a laid-back atmosphere, inventive cocktails and exceptional food inspired their expansion to Cheltenham, a town with a vibe that simply felt like the perfect match for their ethos.

The premises, a characterful Georgian townhouse situated on Cambray Place, won them over immediately. On entering the restaurant, which is tucked away slightly downstairs in the basement, the atmosphere is stylish and intimate with dark wood panelling, low-lighting and cosy corners – the perfect place to enjoy a prime steak accompanied by a glass of red wine.

And it is the steaks that have given this eatery such a strong reputation. Their supplier Bristol butcher, Nigel Buxton, is renowned for his Himalayan salt chamber where he dry-ages his beef, and The Ox give this quality meat a starring role on their menu by cooking it to perfection in their charcoal Josper oven.

It's not all about the steaks, however, as the chefs are given freedom to be creative with local and seasonal ingredients. They have been warmly welcomed by the foodie community of Cheltenham and are establishing some strong relationships with local suppliers, for example by having some great Cotswold beers on the drinks menu.

"It's got the feel of a neighbourhood bar," explains Nathan Lee, one of the founders, "thanks to how warmly it has been received by the local residents and businesses. It has also got the brilliant addition of a terrace, which is a great spot for people who just want to pop in for a drink at any time of day."

However, there is no denying that the food is at the heart of everything they do, from the famed steaks, innovative small plates and charcuterie boards to those delectable desserts. Let's not forget the Sunday roasts, too – the roast beef rib-eye is quickly becoming the talk of Cheltenham.

Early Bird, 14
Served 5pm 7pm
with bearnaise or peppercorn sauce
Bites
Toast

The Ox

DEEP-FRIED PIG'S HEAD, SOFT POACHED EGG, FRISÉE AND BACON SALAD

This dish has become something of a classic at The Ox and has assured itself as a firm favourite with the customers. The recipe is a great example of nose-to-tail eating, using parts of the animal which often go to waste. As a result it's reasonably cheap to make, combining big punchy flavours with beautiful presentation to create an elegant, yet incredibly tasty dish.

Preparation time: 1 hour, plus chilling | Cooking time: 5 hours | Serves 4

Ingredients

For the pig's head croquette:

Half a pig's head, split down the middle, with all the whiskers burnt off with a blow torch

2 carrots

2 small onions

2 sticks celery

4 sprigs thyme

2 tbsp Dijon mustard

Small bunch of chives, finely chopped

3 banana shallots, finely chopped

Flour, for coating

2 eggs, beaten

100g panko breadcrumbs

Salt and pepper

Oil, for frying

To serve:

Smoked streaky bacon, cut into lardons

4 free-range eggs

1 frisée lettuce, trimmed

Simple vinaigrette

2 pickled onions, sliced

Method

Preheat the oven to 120°c. Cut the ears off the pig's head and put the pig's head in a tray face-side up with the carrots, onions, celery and thyme, and pour in enough water to cover the vegetables. Cover with baking parchment then two layers of foil pressed round the rim to create a seal. Cook in the oven for 5 hours.

Remove the foil from the tray and allow to cool slightly before transferring the pig's head to a clean tray. Starting with the cheeks, remove the flesh from the pig's head – you want a ratio of about one-third fat to two-thirds meat. There are all sorts of morsels on the head (the tongue, cheeks, and some particularly good meat behind the eyes), be bold and you will be rewarded.

Add the mustard, chives and diced shallot and season generously with salt and plenty of black pepper. Stir the mix with a large spoon to combine ingredients and taste for a final seasoning.

Roll the mix into logs with cling film and put into the fridge to set. Your logs should be about 5cm in diameter but don't stress it too much. Once set, slice into rounds of about 1cm. Place some flour in one bowl, the beaten eggs in another and the breadcrumbs in a third. Coat the pig's head rounds in the flour, then the egg, then the breadcrumbs. Refrigerate.

To cook and serve

Fry the bacon lardons until crispy. Shallow-fry the croquettes over a medium heat until golden and crispy. Keep warm.

Soft poach the eggs in water and transfer to a tray lined with some J-cloth. Season with salt and pepper.

Dress the frisée with a little vinaigrette and toss in the bacon and pickled onion. Place a poached egg on top of the warm pigs head croquette and serve with the dressed salad. Enjoy!

The Ox
CAMBRAY CONFERENCE

Short and rich, this cocktail gives a Cotswolds twist to a New York classic, The Conference by Brian Miller, which appeared on the menu at Death & Co in Manhattan circa 2008 and comprises two different whiskies and two brandies to create an Old Fashioned style drink. Whilst the Cambray Conference uses Mr. Miller's for inspiration, the flavours are wholly different but perfectly suited to enjoy whilst propping up the bar at the end of a meat filled dinner!

Blending time: 2 weeks | Preparation time: 5 minutes | Serves 1

Ingredients

20ml Woodford Reserve bourbon

20ml Jamesons whiskey

10ml Trois Rivieres rhum agricole

5ml Quiquiriqui mezcal

2 drops walnut tincture

1 dash Chocolate/Angostura bitter blend

5ml Demerara syrup

For the walnut tincture:

150g walnuts

Rye vodka

Method

Blend the four spirits in a glass bottle for at least two weeks before going onto the bar to be used - this smoothens the mix and helps harmonise all the flavours.

For the walnut tincture

Toast 150g of walnuts and steep in rye vodka. The rye base helps give a slight pepperiness to the tincture and the higher the ABV the better as it will draw out more of the flavour. Use enough vodka to cover the walnuts, using a large Kilner jar. Leave this to steep for approximately 24 hours at room temperature though keep an eye on it at the latter stage as the mixture can start to take on a milky texture - you don't want this to happen. When the walnut flavour has developed filter the liquid through muslin cloth to remove any particles. Discard the walnuts (makes for a great addition to a carrot cake)! You will be left with approximately 150ml of your walnut tincture as the nuts will have soaked up some of the vodka.

To make the bitter blend simply mix equal parts Angostura bitters and Bitter Truth Chocolate bitters.

For the syrup

Use 2 parts Demerara sugar to 1 part cold water, put on a low heat in a pan and stir occasionally to dissolve the sugar - do not boil.

To make the cocktail

Add 60ml of the bottled spirits to a mixing glass along with the tincture, bitter blend and syrup and stir with plenty of good quality ice to chill, mix and slightly dilute the ingredients.

A fine BOUQUET

Prithvi in Cheltenham has broken the mould. Expertly combining the experience of fine dining with South Asian flavours, its no wonder they've achieved accolades to rank alongside some of the country's best Michelin-starred establishments.

Working in an Indian restaurant fresh from leaving school (incidentally on the premises where Prithvi now stands), owner Jay Rahman has experienced the industry full circle; honing his skills along the way at prestigious hotels and top restaurants. His experience enabled him to achieve the perfect balance when it came to opening his own place back in 2012.

"I wanted to challenge the concept of Indian food in the UK. Nothing had changed since the 1960's there's a more fulfilling experience to had"

Prithvi's menu delicately combines sub-continental spices and wholesome cooking with premium British produce. Each dish is presented with a detail to attention akin to any fine French or British restaurant anywhere in the country.

Their suppliers are carefully selected for their quality, locality, and sustainability, with menus adapting to reflect the seasons -it's unlikely you will find scallops, venison, halibut or Guinea fowl in your average restaurant.

And it's not just the food that receives exceptional attention; guests are looked after far beyond the last bite.

"The experience doesn't end when the guest leaves," says Jay. "Whether they come in the next week or six months down the line, it's a continuation and f the experience. I respond to all emails and feedback personally and with the same care and consideration as I would to someone dining."

This mantra has not gone unnoticed either, with Prithvi featured among the top industry names for numerous awards, for instance it was sixth out of 100 in the Travellers' Choice Fine Dining Awards, amongst the likes of the Fat Duck, L'Enclume and Adam's. In 2016 they were also number six in the list of top ten list of restaurants in the country on Trip Advisor.

"To be associated with such highly regarded restaurants is a testament to our endeavours. Indian food is often relegated to the lower rung of the ladder, but the calibre of the Prithvi' experience has been recognised amongst prestigious and acclaimed restaurants. To be with, and even surpassing, restaurants with Michelin Stars is humbling, but we're are proud with everything we have achieved thus far"

PR|THVI
PRITHVI

Prithvi

HALIBUT WITH BLACK MUSTARD JUS

A staple in the north eastern region of Bangladesh, the jus is fantastic with all sea fare. The halibut is a meaty and fragrant fish that lends well to the strong and earthy roasted mustard. This dish is best accompanied by a root vegetable, we chose the broccoli tenderstems as a seasonal accompaniment.

Preparation time: 15 minutes | Cooking time: 30 minutes | Serves 4

Ingredients

For the mustard jus:

¾ tbsp roasted black mustard seeds, crushed

4 tbsp rapeseed oil

6 garlic cloves, chopped

1 ½ medium onions, sliced

Table salt

3 bay leaves

½-1 tsp turmeric

½-1 tsp coriander

½-1 tsp curry powder

½-1 tsp chilli powder

Fresh coriander

For the halibut:

1 tsp rapeseed oil

½ tsp turmeric

½ tsp coriander

½ tsp curry powder

½ tsp chilli powder

4 halibut fillets, boned and skinned

Sea salt

For the broccoli:

240g tenderstem broccoli

Butter

Sea salt

Black pepper, crushed

¼ tsp curry powder

Method

Prepare the black mustard jus beforehand. Lightly toast the black mustard seeds in a dry skillet then crush by hand using a pestle and mortar.

In a deep pan heat the rapeseed oil on a low heat, when warm (it will not work if the oil is too hot) add the garlic and let it lightly brown. Add the onions and stir. Add ¼ tablespoon of salt to taste and stir often, making sure it doesn't catch the bottom of the pan. Drop in the bay leaves.

Once the onions have lost most of their liquid start adding hot water, half a cup at a time. Once the water has reduced add another half a cup. Do this four times or until the onions and garlic have become soft.

Now add the spices – use ½ teaspoon if you like it mild or a whole one if you prefer it spicier. Stir often and don't let it catch the bottom of the pan. Keep adding a small amount of hot water to stop the spices from burning. The spices will take on a vibrant colour.

Add ¾ of a tablespoon of the crushed black mustard seeds and stir in for 5-6 minutes. Add 1½ cups of hot water, raise the heat to medium, cover and let it simmer for 10 minutes.

Lastly add the freshly chopped coriander and stir in.

For the halibut

In a flat dish add the rapeseed oil, turmeric, coriander, curry powder, chilli powder, sea salt and mix using a teaspoon.

Add the halibut and softly massage the fish all over with the marinade. You can fry the fish as soon as you're ready – there's no need to leave it to marinate for this dish.

Shallow fry the halibut with rapeseed oil on a medium to low heat. For a crunchy crust cook for 3-4 minutes on each side to get a crunchy crust or 2 to 3 minutes if you prefer it softer.

For the broccoli

Boil the broccoli in hot water for 2 minutes. Add to a colander and run under cold tap water or place in a bowl with ice and water to refresh.

In a skillet pan add a knob of butter and the tenderstems. Add sea salt, crushed black pepper and, most importantly, a sprinkling of curry powder for 3-4 minutes on a medium heat.

To serve

On a deep plate add the jus and place the halibut on top and the tender stems on the side.

After years spent enjoying coffee the Aussie way, when Vikki Hodge and husband Rob moved back to the UK, they decided to bring the style with them.

Determined to do things properly, before leaving the land Down Under, Vikki and Rob did their research, meeting up with industry experts and gaining insight into the art of running a roastery.

Fast forward a few months and Rave Coffee had boiled over from a small shed operation to a unit on an industrial estate, complete with café overlooking the whole roasting process.

"The glass partition shows we've nothing to hide," says Vikki. "There's no dark, secret recipe. We want people to see what we're doing, to know how their coffee is produced."

And it's not just the roasting process that they're transparent about. A good portion of the profits are reinvested into the company, as they seek out the top range of environmentally friendly and sustainably grown beans.

Brooke Purdon, head of coffee, explains the process: "We choose the tastiest coffee first and foremost, then look at the social, sustainable aspects, whether the workers are paid fairly and that the farmers are actually getting the money. Then we look at the relationships with the importers and exporters – they have to be transparent. We like to see whether there are provisions like day care, schools, and lodgings for the workers. Basically, coffee is always better when the workers are happy, which is why we pay over the odds."

After going through such lengths to acquire the very best beans, they need to be processed with precision and care: "Coffee is an incredibly complex fruit, with more aromatic compounds than wine or whiskey," says Brooke. "So we try and find traits in each bean we want to showcase and emphasise. Crop after crop can differ with the seasons; the altitude, humidity and weather helps develop the fruit year after year, which is why it will always taste different."

The team's passion for speciality coffee is not something they keep to themselves; offering regular free training and demonstrations to their customers and wholesalers, they ensure everyone they work with is as excited about both the process and the end product as they are.

Ultimately, it's feedback from customers that determines where they get the beans from. With this unique and innovative approach, it's no wonder they've bagged a two star Great Taste award, found their coffee adorn the pages of glossy magazines like Vogue and Tatler, while The Sunday Times marked their subscription as a 'must have' for Christmas 2016.

Rave Coffee
RAVE COFFEE
WWW.RAVECOFFEE.CO.UK TEL: 01285 651884
PAPUA NEW GUINE
RAW ARABIC
FUDGE
RAVE'S BLEND
TASTING NOTES

Rave Coffee
UPGRADED CAFETIERE

We've chosen the cafetière for a few reasons but chief among them is it is the closest brew method to resemble 'cupping' (no sniggering you lot). Cupping is an industry standard for evaluating and tasting coffee and the method is the same all across the world whether you are a coffee farmer, exporter, broker, roaster or café owner. Here's our take on the humble cafetière:

Grind: gritty, coarser than sand when rubbed between the fingers

Coffee/water ratio: 60g per litre of water (scale up and down as necessary) | Total brew time: 9-10 minutes

Ingredients

60g of favourite coffee grind

1l water

Equipment:

Cafetière

Method

Boil the kettle and preheat your cafetière with hot water for 30 seconds while you set up your coffee dose or grind your beans.

Drain the water from the cafetière and set it on a kitchen scale if available and tare. Boil the kettle again.

Add your coffee to the cafetière and then your freshly boiled water, we aim for 93 degrees, but 10 seconds off the boil will suffice.

Ensure all the coffee grounds are saturated with water when you're pouring, don't be shy, slosh it in up to the desired weight of water.

Leave this for 4 minutes with the lid off and then grab two tablespoons. This is where we divert from normal cafetière routine and delve into cupping territory!

Using the back of the spoon break the crust of the coffee and gently stir a few times. Indulge in some appreciation of the aroma as you do so.

Leave again for 5 minutes (note we have not pressed or plunged!) for the ground coffee to settle at the bottom and optimum temperature to be reached.

Place the lid and mesh onto the cafetière but do not press, just let it rest on the surface of the coffee.

Gently pour into cups and savour a sweet, balanced cup of coffee.

Pat yourself on the back and make another.

Special EVENTS

A specialist events catering company based in the Cotswolds.

Since 1996, Relish Events have established a reputation in the South-West and all around the UK, working with prestigious clients, showgrounds and other venues to provide high-quality catering and service.

In the past 20 years, Relish has established long-standing relationships within the local community as well as with high-profile clients and venues. For the Relish team, it all comes down to their love of food, from the bespoke menu design and table styling to the tasting and then the final extravaganza! The executive chef Rob and his team pride themselves on being real foodies with a huge interest in fresh, locally sourced food within the Cotswolds.

As you would expect, catering comes in all different styles and sizes. Relish now operates multiple fixed venues around the Cotswolds, providing hospitality at high profile outdoor events, with a dedicated team of event organisers.

One of the things Relish enjoys the most is being part of great celebrations from weddings to big birthday feasts! They work with beautiful wedding locations within the Cotswolds such as The Great Tythe Barn, Paintworks Event Space and surrounding areas, Winkworth Farm, Bittenham Springs and Cirencester Park Polo Club. Relish never underestimate the importance of catering for such pinnacle celebrations, and their specialist catering team create culinary masterpieces that wow guests from Italian feasts to American-style pop-up stalls. They take the time to create a unique experience for all customers by working with them to devise a personalised menu to match their special event.

Relish work at some of the UK's most prestigious outdoor events including Badminton Horse Trials, Blenheim Horse Trials, The Game Fair, Althorp Literature Festival, Cheltenham Literature Festival, Hay Festival, RHS Malvern Spring Show and Royal International Air Tattoo. Ever professional, they aim to meet client needs to the exact detail and are renowned for being specialist outdoor event caterers.

On the other side of the spectrum are the private parties, where customers can choose a bespoke menu design just for them! These include office celebrations and birthday bashes, garden parties, private homes and seasonal events, as well as venues such as the Gateway Café at Cotswold Water Park and Cirencester Park Polo Club.

Understanding the details of each occasion allows Relish to shape their management to each event, meticulously plan and coordinate, whether it is a dinner party for ten or an outdoor festival with thousands of people!

Relish

ROAST PHEASANT, BUTTERMILK LEG, SPELT RISOTTO, QUINCE, CAVOLO NERO AND TRUFFLES

Great Britain has some of the finest game in the world. This autumn/winter dish marries fabulous seasonal ingredients with the delicious well hung pheasant.

Preparation time: 2 hours | Cooking time: 45 minutes | Serves 4

Ingredients

For the pheasant breast:

4 pheasant breasts

1 British black truffle

8 thin slices pancetta

Oil, for frying

Salt and pepper

For the KFP (Kentucky fried pheasant):

4 pheasant legs

300ml buttermilk

1 egg, beaten

4 serving spoons cornflour

4 serving spoons plain flour

1 tbsp onion powder

1 tsp garlic powder

1 tsp mustard powder

1 tsp salt

1 tsp black pepper

For the risotto:

50g dried porcini mushrooms

1 leek, trimmed and diced

75g butter

Olive oil, for cooking

75g mixed seeds

2 cloves garlic

200g chestnut mushrooms

200g pearled spelt

100g Sussex Charmer

For the garnish:

Cavolo nero, boiled

2 quince, roasted

Method

For the pheasant breast

Preheat the oven to 200°c. Fillet the pheasant breasts, season well, grate a little black truffle on the inside of the breasts and wrap two breasts together with the pancetta. Repeat so you have used all four breasts to create two pheasant ballotines. Pan-fry for a few minutes to give some colour all over, then cook in the hot oven for 15-20 minutes until a core temperature of 58°c is reached. Rest for 10 minutes.

For the KFP (Kentucky Fried Pheasant)

Fillet the legs and remove any feather bones. Mix the buttermilk and egg together in one bowl, and mix the dry ingredients together in another. Soak the legs in the buttermilk and egg, then roll into the dry ingredients. Preheat a deep-fryer to 170°c and deep fry for 8 minutes.

For the risotto

Rehydrate the dried mushrooms in 500ml of boiling water; this will make a mushroom stock. Fry the diced leek in little of the butter and some olive oil. Add the seeds, garlic and chestnut mushrooms and continue to sweat down. Add the spelt and stock and simmer until the grain is tender; add more water if needed. To finish, add the remaining butter and the grated cheese at the end, whilst still simmering, and stir to a glossy creamy finish. Season.

To serve

Prepare the garnishes (boil the cavolo nero and roast the quince) and serve the risotto with the pheasant breasts and KFP. Garnish with the cavolo nero and quince and serve.

Rising STARS

Part of National Star, Star Bistro serves some of the finest food in the Cotswolds. Based at two locations in Ullenwood and Royal Crescent, this unique eatery also offers young people with disabilities the opportunity to gain work experience and realise their aspirations.

One of two inspirational dining destinations from National Star, Star Bistro at Ullenwood is located on The Cotswold Way in the grounds of Ullenwood Manor. It opened in 2012, and operating in partnership with National Star, it enables learners to work alongside an experienced hospitality team within a bustling restaurant environment.

Its location in the heart of the Cotswolds enables Star Bistro at Ullenwood to offer tempting dishes created from seasonal and local ingredients – from breakfasts and morning coffees to light lunches and afternoon teas. The space is available to hire for events and can accommodate both private parties and corporate events, as well as a variety of special events throughout the year.

The successful venue at Ullenwood has been joined by another eatery at Royal Crescent. A hidden gem tucked away in the heart of a regency terrace in Cheltenham, this restaurant is, like its sister, no ordinary bistro! Spoilt for choice with the range of fresh produce available on its doorstep, the kitchen transforms local and seasonal goodies into beautiful breakfasts, light bites, tempting cakes and a delicious lunch menu. They even offer a 'to go' menu for those who want to grab something tasty to eat on the run.

Star Bistro at Royal Crescent can be hired for parties of up to 60 people, and the bistro also boasts the Harcourt Room, a space that has become popular with small private events. As it seats up to 20 guests, it makes the perfect spot to host business meetings or get the family together for a special occasion. The talented Star Bistro team offer outside catering options, too.

Both Star Bistros have become firm favourites in Cheltenham. Rave reviews highlight the excellent dishes and service, as well as the positive ethos around supporting local producers and the creation of a supportive workplace for people with disabilities, enabling them to learn valuable new skills.

Star Bistro
StarBistro

Star Bistro

MALTED STOUT AND OAT TART

A love of coffee and craft beer inspired this dish. It started as a 'coffee and biscuit' idea. It's a cross between a treacle tart and a parkin, but not as heavy as either and the porter adds a wonderful bitterness to the ice cream.

Preparation time: 15 minutes | Cooking time: 40 minutes | Serves 4

Ingredients

For the tart:

330ml bottle of coffee porter (we use Stroud Brewery's Sumatran Coffee Porter)

1 tsp coffee extract

50g unsalted butter

300g golden syrup

80g malt extract

50g double cream

1 egg and 2 egg yolks

1 tbsp freshly squeezed lemon juice

150g oats

For the coffee porter ice cream:

1 tsp coffee extract

2 tsp Kahlua coffee liqueur

90g sugar

100g egg yolks

500ml milk

Vanilla pod and seeds

30g instant coffee powder

200g double cream

For the coffee honeycomb:

100g caster sugar

3 tbsp glucose syrup

2 tbsp honey

1½ tsp bicarbonate of soda

1 tsp instant coffee powder

Method

For the tart

Place the coffee porter in a pan and reduce by two-thirds. Measure out 100g of the reduced liquid and add the coffee extract. Reserve the rest of the reduced porter for the ice cream.

Melt the butter. Add the golden syrup, malt extract, double cream and the 100g reduced coffee porter. Heat until melted. Quickly whisk in the egg, egg yolks and lemon juice. Mix in the oats.

Place into a lined tin (10x10cm) and leave to set and firm up for 15-20 minutes. Meanwhile, preheat the oven to 170°c.

Bake the tart for 10-15 minutes, until golden brown, set and firm but soft to the touch. Leave to cool before cutting.

For the coffee porter ice cream

Reduce the reserved reduced coffee porter down even further to 20g and add the coffee extract and coffee liqueur. Whisk the sugar and yolks until pale. Put the rest of the ingredients in a pan with the reduced porter and heat to just below boiling. Slowly whisk on to the yolks and then return to the pan. Cook slowly, stirring constantly until mixture reaches 80°c, then allow to cool and chill the mixture until cold. Churn in an ice cream machine and store in the freezer until ready to use.

For the coffee honeycomb

Bring the sugar, glucose and honey slowly to the boil and cook gently until the mixture reaches 160°c. Quickly whisk in the bicarbonate of soda and the coffee powder. Pour on to a silicon mat to set until hard. Break into pieces.

To serve

Gently warm the tart. Place on a cool plate with shards of honeycomb and a scoop of ice cream. I serve mine with a vanilla bean espuma mousse and lemon balm micro leaf.

Sumptuously SUSTAINABLE

Based in a working pottery, The Straw Kitchen is a uniquely sustainable place to eat thanks to its owner's uncompromising commitment to the local environment and seasonal produce.

What was once a derelict barn is today home to a charming, low-impact café which has been slowly and lovingly created by Maia Keeling and Christine Bottine. Set within the grounds of Maia's parents' traditional Cotswolds pottery, Whichford Pottery, the café is a celebration of the environment that surrounds them.

When they decided to open a low-impact café, they had no intention of doing anything by halves. The build took a year, and Christine and Maia learnt many traditional techniques as they constructed their building using environmentally friendly materials. The walls are made from straw bales, which give the café its name, and there is no concrete in the building's structure at all. Reclaimed bricks, timber and windows were used, and the floors are insulated with recycled glass blocks. Raw clay from the pottery allowed them to make their own clay plaster and natural clay paint.

However going green didn't start and end with the building's structure – it runs through the ethos of everything that happens at The Straw Kitchen. The menu has a couple of regular elements on it, but most if it changes depending on what is in season. They work with their neighbouring pig farmers, Paddock Farm Butchery to source meat for their renowned brunches, buy veggies from nearby farm shops and get all their dairy produce from the milkman, The Country Dairy, who lives just up the hill. The ice cream is made by their friend Lance from Herbalicious Ice Creams, who uses home-grown fruits and seasonal flowers to concoct unusual combinations such as rosemary and rose or lemon balm and lemon verbena.

Vegetarian options outweigh meaty dishes, which is a reflection of their belief in eating less meat where possible, and preferring to source the very best, sustainably reared, local meat when they do use it.

Alongside their staples (think local bacon sarnies with homemade beetroot relish, eggs on homemade bread or chorizo and feta on toast), they draw inspiration from all over the world, from 17th-century England through to Japan and Vietnam via France and the Middle East. They love to travel and always return with a plethora of recipe ideas!

For Christine, it is this diversity that sets them apart: "What our customers really like is that they can come one week and have our take on freshly made Vietnamese spring rolls, the next week a 48-hour slow-cooked pulled shoulder of pork cooked in harissa and pomegranate molasses, and the next week a lush frittata with our own home-grown cherry tomatoes and courgettes."

The Straw Kitchen

The Straw Kitchen

OKONOMIYAKI: A VERY ENGLISH JAPANESE PANCAKE

We love revisiting street food classics from around the world, giving them our own English twist. This delectable treat from Osaka is one of our customers' favourites, for its quirky finish and myriad potential fillings. Beware, some flipping is required! You can replace the cabbage, turnip and carrot with any other grated or shredded vegetables you have in the bottom of your fridge. Check online or in certain supermarkets for the pickled ginger and seaweed, they are a delicious bonus.

Preparation time: 30 minutes | Cooking time: 10 minutes | Serves 1 as a main or 2 as a starter

Ingredients

For the pancake:

100g flour (can be gluten-free)
1 free-range egg
100ml vegetable or chicken stock
2 tbsp ginger, peeled and grated
1 turnip, grated
1 carrot, grated
Small handful mint, shredded
2 tbsp rape seed oil
2 garlic cloves
3 spring onions, finely chopped
20g frozen peas
100g Savoy cabbage, shredded

For the onion, carrot and ginger pickle:

100ml rice wine vinegar
1 tbsp caster sugar
3 tbsp ginger, diced
1 onion, thinly sliced
1 carrot, diced

For the topping:

1 tbsp pickled sushi ginger
2 tbsp mayonnaise
Seaweed flakes

Method

For the pancake

Whisk the flour, egg and stock together until it forms a thick batter, just thicker than double cream. Add a touch more stock if you think it's still too thick after whisking. You can use a gluten-free flour mix here, as it will still act as a binder for your batter. Mix in the ginger, grated turnip, carrot and mint with a fork.

Pour half the oil into a 20cm frying pan (an omelette pan is ideal) and wait for it to heat up. When ready, throw in the garlic, half the spring onions and the frozen peas. When the garlic starts to brown, add the cabbage. Cook for about 1 minute until just soft; you still want a bit of a crunch left in it.

Add the rest of the oil and pour in the batter, making sure it has coated all the cabbage and pea mix. Cook for about 2 minutes on a medium heat. When the edges look darker, slip a knife under the mix to loosen it. Don't worry if the mix still looks runny.

Here comes the exciting flip! Grab a plate larger than your pan, and, after checking that you've loosened the bottom of the pancake in the pan, flip it over onto the plate. If the top sticks, just scrape it off and add it to your mix again.

Slip it all back into the frying pan for about 2 minutes to cook the underside until it feels firm. Meanwhile, make the pickle…

For the onion, carrot and ginger pickle

Pour the vinegar into a saucepan on a low heat and stir in the sugar until it has dissolved. Add the diced ginger, onion and carrot. This will easily keep for 1 week in the fridge.

For the topping

Sprinkle with the rest of the spring onions, your onion, carrot and ginger pickle, the pickled ginger and seaweed flakes. To finish it off in true Japanese style, put the mayonnaise in a piping bag and pipe a lattice all over the pancake. For a simpler finish, just blob the mayo over the pancake! Hey presto, here you have your own okonomiyaki!

Fresh from THE FARMS

Stroud Farmers' Market is well known as one of the biggest, busiest and most popular farmers' markets in the UK – an enticing feast of sights, aromas, colours and sounds.

A farmers' market is often the heart of a community, a place where people can come together and celebrate the diverse array of things that are grown, produced and created in the local area. From the mouthwatering smells of freshly cooked food to the lively sounds of people enjoying themselves, a trip to the local farmers' market can be a feast for all the senses.

Stroud is one place that boasts an exemplary market. Launched in July 1999 as a result of Stroud's Community Planning conferences of the 1990s, Stroud Farmers' Market was one of the country's first farmers' markets. It began as a way of regenerating the town centre and providing a new direct sales market for local farmers and food producers.

Although it was initially planned to be a monthly market, it didn't take long before it became a twice-a-month occurrence. It proved extremely popular from the outset and was embraced by the people of Stroud. Relationships were forged between the market, its customers and the local farmers and producers. By 2005 it had become a weekly market – the first in Gloucestershire to do so – and it has been happening weekly in Stroud ever since!

It is still one of only a handful of farmers' markets in the country to take place regularly every week, which is testament to the dedication of both the traders and the customers. A huge number of people do their big weekly shop at the market as it is the perfect place to access a full range of good-quality local produce.

Today, 18 years since the market began life, it remains at the heart of Stroud's community. Week in, week out, the market showcases the produce of up to 60 local food businesses from Stroud and the surrounding region. Certified as a genuine farmers' market by FARMA, customers to the market can be assured of the local provenance of the vast range of foods available.

Stroud Farmers' Market

The market has accumulated numerous awards over the years, including the FARMA Farmers' Market of the Year twice, The Farm Food and Deli Awards Best Farmers' Market and BBC Food and Farming Food Market of the Year. It has also been the focus of many television appearances thanks to its intoxicating atmosphere which is a veritable feast for all the senses.

Many of the traders have been coming to Stroud Farmers' Market for many years, and they report how important the market is to them. They enjoy the vibrant atmosphere and engaging with the local customers.

The balance of traders at the market creates a vibrant festival of colours, sounds, smells and tastes that entices you around the packed market square and out into the surrounding streets. At its core the market has a strong showing of primary producers; farmers and growers bringing their raw produce to market.

There are four vegetable growers (five in season), five meat farmers, soft fruit and top fruit growers in season, dairy and cheesemakers, eggs, beekeepers, mushroom suppliers, flower growers and nurseries with plants for the gardens. The array of traders means that shoppers have an impressive range of produce to choose from and provides a glimpse into the bounty of the Cotswolds countryside. The colourful displays offer a vibrant view of the season, as the produce available will change from one month to the next.

Add to this the wide array of artisan food producers and it is easy to understand why Stroud Farmers' Market has become such a foodie paradise. Stall are packed with such delights as hand-made pies, fine wines, charcuterie, preserves, sauces, cakes, breads, beers and ciders, so it is possible to buy everything you need in one visit.

A legendary selection of street food stalls is also present, which fills the air with delicious aromas of foods from all around the world. Add a final sprinkling of local makers with wood, wool, leather, ceramics and more (plus the adjacent Threadneedle Flea Market) and you can see why the market has become so popular over the years.

Entertainment from talented locals is a regular feature, and the market café in the square is a great place to rest your legs and soak up the atmosphere. Stroud farmers' market runs every Saturday throughout the year (except between Christmas and New Year) from 9am to 2pm in The Cornhill Market Square.

Stroud Farmers' Market

Stroud PROUD

Stroud is a hotbed of innovation and art... and Stroud Brewery have crafted a range of organic and vegan beers that reflect their surroundings in every way.

With barley grown on the surrounding Cotswolds hills, the beers that are carefully produced at Stroud Brewery are as local as they can possibly be. Managing Director Greg Pilley set up the brewery having always had what he describes as "a disproportionate interest in beer" and a lifelong ambition to run his own brewery.

However Stroud Brewery stands out as something quite special, not only thanks to the distinctive beers it produces but in the way the company is run. Their ambition is to produce the highest quality beers with care for people and planet.

They have crafted a range of organic and vegan beers made with locally grown barley. Most of the beers are brewed to organic standards and are certified by the Soil Association. They use craft and small-scale suppliers, for example malt from Warminster Maltings, which might cost them more but reflects their core principals.

Spent grain goes to feed local cattle and pigs, and spent hops go for compost. The use of lightweight bottles is just one of the ways they try to keep their energy use down where possible. None of their products are available through the multiple retailers, and are sold largely to pubs within the Cotswolds and independent retailers across the UK. They are passionate about supporting their local economy, whether that means borrowing money from local people rather than banks or choosing to spend within the area. Being part of a thriving community is a huge part of what makes the team at Stroud Brewery tick.

The largest range of Stroud Brewery beers can be found at their very own bar. It is a place where it is easy to meet new people – it's informal and family-friendly, and it is open Thursday, Friday and Saturday evenings, with live acoustic music every Saturday. People describe it as a real hub of the community where the freshly made pizzas are washed down by the excellent Stroud Brewery beers. The local and organic policy extends to the food in their bar, too, of course. Organic, local and delicious!

STROUD
Brewery
STROUD
Stroud Brewery
Organic Ale
4%
STROUD
Brewery
Alederflower
Organic Pale Ale
4.9%
No 23

No 23 Bar & Bistro

TOM LONG MARINATED PORK CHOPS, ALEDERFLOWER BRAISED CABBAGE AND A SWEET POTATO PURÉE

This recipe from No 23 gives Stroud Brewery's Tom Long and Alederflower starring roles. No 23 is a small but very popular independent Bistro in Stroud, which was created 5 years ago to celebrate the love of good food and good company. It has consistently been voted the #1 restaurant in the Stroud area and in the top 1% of Cotswold restaurants. The No 23 team specialises in seasonal and Mediterranean fare, great seafood, vegan and tapas dishes, and both local and international beverages.

Preparation time: 30 minutes, plus 4 hours marinating | Cooking time: 30 minutes | Serves 2

Ingredients

For the pork chops:

1 bottle of Stroud Brewery's Tom Long

1 tbsp coarse salt

3 tsp ground black pepper

5 fresh sage leaves

1 onion, finely diced

3 tbsp pomegranate molasses

1 tbsp Worcestershire sauce

3 tbsp dark muscovado sugar

2 pork chops

For the sweet potato purée:

2 medium sweet potatoes, peeled and chopped into bite-size pieces

2 knobs of butter

40ml double cream

Salt and pepper

For the Alederflower braised cabbage:

1 onion, finely diced

A splash of oil, for cooking

1 tbsp garlic purée

1 can of Alederflower

1 tsp wholegrain mustard

1 tbsp brown sugar

1 tbsp Worcestershire sauce

1 white cabbage, shredded

Method

For the pork chops

To make the pork chop marinade, in a large bowl combine the Tom Long, coarse salt, black pepper, sage leaves, diced onion, molasses, Worcestershire sauce, muscovado sugar and 330ml of water. Stir well until the salt and sugar are dissolved.

Place your pork chops in a large sealed container, pour over the marinade and refrigerate for at least 4 hours (longer if you have time).

For the sweet potato purée

Put the chopped sweet potato into a pan of salted boiling water and simmer until they are soft enough to mash.

Meanwhile, back to the pork chops

Preheat your griddle pan to a medium-high heat, and splash in some oil. Remove your chops from the marinade, being careful to ensure you have removed enough liquid to avoid it burning your hot pan. Grill the chops for 10 minutes on each side until cooked, then leave them to rest for around 5 minutes.

For the Alederflower braised cabbage

Whilst your pork chops are resting, take a medium saucepan, add the diced onion with a little oil and garlic purée, and sweat for 2 minutes. Stir in your Alederflower, wholegrain mustard, brown sugar and Worcestershire sauce. Add the shredded cabbage and cook for 7-8 minutes or until soft. Drain and serve when ready.

To serve

Once your sweet potatoes are soft drain, add the butter, cream and salt and pepper to taste. Using a hand-held blender blitz until you have a smooth consistency. Serve all together with a cold glass of Stroud Budding! Enjoy!

There is much more to sweet potatoes than a portion of fries... and The Sweet Potato Spirit Company have been showcasing the extraordinary qualities of their vegetables in their award-winning range of drinks.

The idea to try to create spirits from sweet potatoes all started from a chance conversation in a North Carolina eatery... Cotswolds-based sweet potato growers, importers and exporters were visiting their farms in the USA when someone raised the question, would it be possible to create spirits from these delicious vegetables?

Not one to shy away from a challenge, Garry Smith began work on a plan to take sweet potatoes to new levels. He and his team began by developing a moonshine. The aim was to create something completely different to the products already on the market – this certainly wasn't going to be a firewater, but a top-end-of-the-market drink that would be smooth and flavoursome.

The sweet potatoes would be distilled in copper stills with the same care and attention that they received from the farm. This seed-to-bottle approach is what gives the drinks the edge when it comes to taste and quality – all-natural ingredients, and hand-crafted from scratch.

With a successful moonshine under their belt, the team decided to work on creating a range of products before launching them. They carefully developed the drinks, working out what ingredients might partner well with sweet potatoes to create accessible spirits that people would enjoy drinking. They decided on a spiced rum, orangecello and raspberry liqueur.

Founder of The Sweet Potato Spirit Company, Garry, explains how the inherent sweetness of the potatoes helps to create a refined drinking experience, but doing everything themselves from scratch gives them much more control over the final taste: "It gives us the ability to remove the heads and tails of the spirit in exacting quantities to ensure that only the heart of the spirit is in the bottle." He goes on to explain that the 'heads' are what can often give the burn associated with spirits, and the 'tails' are associated with an unpleasant aftertaste. By removing these waste products they have been able to create really smooth, pleasurable drinks.

They followed the original four products with a London dry gin, plum gin, vodka, toffee apple moonshine, pink marshmallow moonshine and chocolate moonshine with chilli. With a World Food Innovation Award for Best New Artisan Beverage achieved for the initial range in 2016 and medals in three different world spirit competitions, there is much excitement surrounding the new drinks... along with rumours of more awards announcements soon.

PREMIUM
A PURE SPIRIT
HANDMADE
IN
COPPERSTILLS
004
MOON
Shine
A PURE SPIRIT
HANDMADE
IN
COPPERSTILLS
SPICED
RUM
A PURE SPIRIT
HANDMADE
IN
COPPERSTILLS
LIQUEUR
HANDMADE
IN
COPPERSTILLS

DRY GIN
PURE
HANDMADE
IN
COPPERSTILLS

The Sweet Potato Spirit Company
ALL-DAY BREAKFAST MARTINI

Sweet potatoes are so versatile whether in cooking or making spirits. This recipe is a play on the famous Breakfast Martini which originally uses gin, marmalade, lemon juice and triple sec liqueur. We love sharing all the possibilities with sweet potatoes so much that we've included our jam recipe and encourage you to make a day of it. The rewards are sweet.

Preparation time: 5 minutes | Cooking time: 25 minutes | Serves 1

Ingredients

Cubed ice

50ml Sweet Potato Spirits Gin

25ml fresh lemon juice

20ml triple sec

2 tablespoons Sweet Potato and Ginger Jam (see below)

Citrus peel twist

Method

Overfill a martini glass with ice for a couple of minutes to chill the glass. Add the gin (spiced rum works well instead here too!), lemon juice and triple sec to a cocktail shaker. Stir in the sweet potato and ginger jam – a taste test will let you know if you want even more of that lovely sweet potato taste and texture. If you haven't time to make the jam or have already run out of it, marmalade can also be substituted.

Discard the melt water from the martini glass and transfer the ice cubes into the shaker – the more ice the better the resulting drink. Shake vigorously to chill before straining into a martini glass. Garnish with the oils from the citrus by twisting over your cocktail.

To make sweet potato and ginger jam

Place peeled sweet potatoes in a pan with some water and boil until soft. Drain the sweet potatoes and mash. Weigh the sweet potatoes and place in a heavy-based pan with an equal weight of sugar. Place on medium heat and bring to the boil, stirring occasionally. Add freshly grated ginger to taste, reduce the heat to a gentle simmer and cook for at least 10 minutes. Carry on cooking until a desired consistency has been reached. Sterilise some jam jars by boiling them in water. Pour the hot jam into the hot jam jars and leave to cool.

SWEET POTATO
SPICED RUM
PREMIUM

The Sweet Potato Spirit Company

ESPRESSO MARTINI

The Espresso Martini has become one of the most popular bar calls in the last few years – a sophisticated and energising mix of caffeine and alcohol that's become so much easier to make at home now that so many of us have pod machines and quality local cafes. While we agree it's excellent using Sweet Potato Spirits' Vodka we like to shake it up with our Spiced Rum for an added flavour dimension. Which SP are you?

Preparation time: 5 minutes | Serves 1

Ingredients

Cubed ice

2 tsp sugar

1 shot espresso

½ shot coffee liqueur

2 shots Sweet Potato Spirits Spiced Rum

3 coffee beans

Lemon twist (optional)

Method

Overfill a martini glass with ice for a couple of minutes to chill the glass. Dissolve the sugar in the shot of fresh espresso and pour into a cocktail shaker. If you measure the coffee liqueur and Spiced Rum using the same espresso cup before adding these to the shaker, you will get all of the extra flavours found within the espresso crema. Have a quick taste to check if you prefer it sweeter, adding more sugar if required.

Discard the melt water from the martini glass and transfer the ice cubes into the shaker – the more ice the better the resulting drink. Shake vigorously to chill and aerate before straining into a martini glass. Garnish with the coffee beans.

Creating a BUZZ

Husband and wife team Greg and Caroline Saturley are proud owners of The Vault, a beautifully converted old bank in the middle of Nailsworth, The Canteen, a fun and quirky cafe, and The Hog, an award-winning country pub in the village of Horsley.

Each of the three venues owned by Greg and Caroline has its own unique vibe, but there are definite similarities – those tell-tale signs you are in a place that the Saturleys run. There is great attention to detail and a strong ethos of showcasing the very best of local produce, with strong Mediterranean flavours.

Caroline, who was the local midwife for years, and her photographer husband Greg, became interested in running food businesses when they returned from a five-year stint in sunny Cyprus, where Caroline was a midwife. Looking for a new direction, they worked their magic on The Canteen, before being asked by the locals in the next village of Horsley to consider bringing their 'brand' of fun, quirky, delicious food up to the pub. A few years later, the derelict bank came on the market, and the rest is history.

The couple's innovative approach is proving to be very popular. All three places are buzzing, which is thanks to them having been carefully designed to offer something a little different to the area. There is also a strong sense of supporting the local economy.

"Nailsworth is a great place to have a business," says Caroline, "It is really vibrant, with a strong sense of community. It seemed to make sense to keep everything local. We feel we have given a few gifts to Nailsworth. Every day people say they love what we have created, it's great to feel appreciated! We are also able to employ the very best of people from the area, and that created a good, strong team. Everyone knows everyone else in this tight-knit community!"

The newly opened Vault has a great energy, perfect for a cocktail or enjoying dining with a meze feel – there are lots of sharing platters and tasting plates designed for everyone to share.

The Canteen, tucked away in the middle of a mill, has a secluded courtyard and a quirky interior. Using the same local ingredients, everything in The Canteen is homemade. The Turkish Breakfast is legendary and the chocolate brownie is to die for!

The Hog, Pub of the Year for the South West Region (Food and Farming) and situated a mile away up the road in the village of Horsley, is not just a local boozer. It's a great mix of traditional pub fare and imaginative dishes complemented by local beers and some great local bands, too.

Mützig
BIERE D'ALSACE
SPECIALS
Mozzarella + Sun Dried Tomat
Croissant £3.50
Walnut
Gluten free
orange, almond
+ blueberry £3
WHITE chocolate TIFFIN £3
TIPS
Apple + Blackberry streusel £3
plain croissant
THE CANTEEN

The Vault BASQUE CRAB

This beautiful recipe uses a large, live Atlantic crab. Serving the dish in the shell looks stunning.

Preparation time: 25-30 minutes | Cooking time: 1 hour | Serves 4-6

Ingredients

1 large Atlantic crab (1.5-2kg)

4 tbsp olive oil

1 onion, finely chopped

1 red pepper, finely chopped

1 green pepper, finely chopped

1 garlic clove, finely chopped

200g white fish, cooked and flaked

½ cup brandy

½ cup white wine

A pinch of cayenne flakes

1 cup chopped tomatoes

1 tbsp chopped parsley

4 tbsp fine breadcrumbs

2 tbsp butter

Salt and pepper, to taste

Method

Put the live crab into boiling salted water and cook for 35-40 minutes. Drain and leave to cool. Pry off the shells and reserve (cleaned and oiled). Discard the stomach from the crab. Scoop out the soft dark meat and flaky white meat.

In a frying pan heat the olive oil and sauté the onion, peppers and garlic until softened. Add the crab meat and cooked fish to the pan. Add the brandy and wine – ignite and, when the flames die down, add the cayenne, salt, pepper, tomatoes and parsley. Cook for 10 minutes.

Spoon the mixture into the crab shell, and sprinkle the top with the breadcrumbs and the butter. Put under a hot grill or into a preheated oven (190°c) until the tops are browned (5 minutes). Crack the legs and serve with the shell. Enjoy!

Chris White and Purdey Spooner had always dreamed of opening a restaurant to their own personal tastes, little did they know everybody else would enjoy their laid-back approach too.

Knowing the only way he could truly have freedom in what he served was with his own place, chef Chris White jumped at the opportunity to relocate to Cheltenham and open a restaurant. Despite no experience of running a business, Chris and his wife Purdey's determination and passion has resulted in a whirlwind 18 months, culminating in being named amongst The Times' top 25 new restaurants, and bagging the best new restaurant award at The Craft Guild of Chefs Awards.

The reason behind their success, Chris puts down to a simple ethos: "We wanted to create a place where we would be happy to dine at. We strive to give all our customers a really memorable experience; top quality food and fantastic service in a relaxed atmosphere. We like to think The White Spoon is a place where everyone feels comfortable, foodie or not. We provide an atmosphere that suits both formal and informal occasions – an alternative to fine dining."

That's not to say the food isn't remarkable though. Their short menu changes regularly with the seasons and availability of only the finest produce. If a supplier has something exceptional, Chris will often build a whole dish around that one ingredient. Their Sunday lunches are particular favourites too, featuring rare bread meat sourced from Butts Farm and Kelmscott Manor. Although they're primarily known for their food, The White Spoon's drinks menu is equally important, from their inimitable wine list, to their in-house Bloody Mary and specially developed house gin:

"We have partnered with a local distillery and the botanicals used have been specially selected by Chris. It has a simple elegance and a unique garnish consisting of fresh apple, lime leaf and a touch of ground black pepper, giving The White Spoon's G&T its very own identity and taste," explains Purdey.

Actively involved in the community, The White Spoon also host regular nights like 'wine, dine and donate', where customers are encouraged to bring their own bottle for a small corkage fee, which is then donated to a local charity.

Like so many they have visited and enjoyed in the past, Purdey and Chris' aims for the future are firmly rooted in making The White Spoon a destination dining experience. Based on their first few months, it looks like that won't take long to achieve…

THE WHITE SPOON
GIN
Cold distilled under vacuum
Distilled & hand bottled in Cheltenham
ABV 43%
Vol 70cl

THE WHITE SPOON

The White Spoon

BUTTERMILK PANNA COTTA, STRAWBERRY SOUP AND BALSAMIC JELLY PEPPER TUILLE

A twist on a modern day classic dessert, pairing traditional flavours of strawberries, black pepper and balsamic vinegar. Celebrating a very British product, perfect for a summers day.

Preparation time: 4.5 hours including cooling time | Cooking time: 40 minutes | Serves 4

Ingredients

For the buttermilk panna cotta:

80ml milk

22g sugar

¾ gelatine leaf

120g buttermilk

For the balsamic jelly:

50ml balsamic vinegar

50g sugar

50ml water

1g agar agar

For the strawberry soup:

300g strawberries

50g sugar

60ml water

Splash of lime juice

For the pepper tuille:

60g caster sugar

40g glucose

10ml water

Ground black pepper

Method

For the buttermilk panna cotta

Boil the milk and sugar together. Soak the gelatine leaf in cold water for 5 minutes. Add the leaf to the milk and sugar mix and allow to cool. Whisk the buttermilk into the mixture and set in the fridge in 4 round shallow pudding moulds.

For the balsamic jelly

Bring the balsamic vinegar, sugar and water to boil. Whisk in the agar agar and bring back to the boil. Set in a shallow dish – the jelly should be approximately 1cm deep. Once set, turn out and cut into 1cm cubes.

For the strawberry soup

Combine the strawberries, sugar and water in a pan and cook on the hob at 60°c for 30 minutes. Finish with a splash of lime juice.

For the pepper tuille

Combine the caster sugar, glucose and water in a pan and bring to 170°c.

Pour out onto parchment paper and allow to cool. Once cooled, peel off the parchment and blitz in a food processor until it becomes a powder. Sieve onto parchment paper to create a circle 10cm in diameter. Cook at 120°c for 5 minutes then sprinkle with ground black pepper whilst still hot.

To serve

Turn out the panna cottas into the centre of 4 shallow bowls. Dress with the poached strawberries and balsamic jelly around the edge. Place the tuille on top of the panna cotta just before serving.

Pour the strawberry soup around the panna cotta at the table.

Local food HEROES

For a quaint Cotswolds market town, Nailsworth certainly has a far-reaching reputation when it comes to being something of a gastronomic hot spot – and much of this comes down to the highly celebrated independent retailer William's Food Hall & Oyster Bar.

Set up by William Beeston back in 1975, this renowned delicatessen and fish market has since been credited for literally 'putting Nailsworth on the map', transforming the Gloucestershire market town from quiet backwater to the celebrated foodie haven it has become today.

Today, under the guidance of head chef Steve Rawicki, it is a place to enjoy first-rate seafood, from freshly shucked oysters to whole Dover sole, accompanied by a glass of wine perhaps. It is also one of the most inspiring places to shop, with fresh fish and seafood from the British coastline, specially selected cheeses, charcuterie and terrines, and a vibrant selection of locally sourced fruits and vegetables, all beautifully displayed.

The William's story began over forty years ago, when William and Rae Beeston opened William's Kitchen at 3 Fountain Street, Nailsworth. Frank Carpenter had a shop there since 1951, selling an array of freshly caught fish from a marble slab in the window, as well as selection of game such as rabbit, fowl and pheasants, usually seen hanging upside down.

William and Rae's business harnessed the success of Frank's shop and swiftly went from strength to strength as a fishmonger, delicatessen and also a caterer, and soon William's Kitchen was attracting attention from all over the region and even from much further afield. William was named as one of Rick Stein's 'Food Heroes' and the shop also gained recognition as one of Matthew Fort's 'Five Favourite Places to Shop'.

In 2014 it was time for William to step down and retire – after an impressive 39 years running his eponymous business, which had now become William's Food Hall & Oyster Bar. It was bought by local family Ed and Helen Playne, who are passionate about continuing the William's story long into the future and maintaining their reputation for culinary excellence in Nailsworth, the Cotswolds and throughout the whole region.

William's Food Hall

William's Food Hall

CHARGRILLED HALIBUT WITH CRAB CRUSHED POTATOES

Freshly caught fish from the William's fish counter pairs beautifully with the flavourful combination of crab and new potatoes. Add a zingy salsa and smooth red pepper sauce for a beautiful medley of tastes and textures.

Preparation time: 30 minutes | Cooking time: 30 minutes | Serves 4

Ingredients

For the salsa:

1 bunch spring onions, diced

1 red pepper, diced

1 yellow pepper, diced

Handful of coriander

50g capers, chopped

50g black olives, chopped

Olive oil

Lemon juice

Salt and pepper

For the pepper sauce:

1 shallot

2 red peppers

1 tsp olive oil

1 tsp smoked paprika

1 sprig thyme

200ml white wine

For the potatoes:

50g butter

1 shallot, peeled and diced

150g crab meat (white and brown)

500g new potatoes, cooked and crushed

50ml lemon juice

Chopped parsley

For the halibut:

4 x 200g halibut steaks

Olive oil, for cooking

Samphire, cooked, to serve

Method

For the salsa

Mix all the ingredients in a bowl, season with salt and pepper and set aside.

For the pepper sauce

Finely chop the shallots and cut the red peppers into small pieces, removing all seeds. Place the shallots in a frying pan with the olive oil and sweat until softened. Then add the peppers and continue to fry for another few minutes. Add the thyme and white wine to the frying pan and simmer for 5 minutes. Then blend the mixture in a food processor until smooth.

For the potatoes

Melt the butter in a saucepan, add the shallots and cook gently until golden brown. Add the crab meat and the crushed potatoes and roughly mix together. Once ready to serve, drizzle with lemon juice and add the chopped parsley.

For the halibut

Pat the halibut dry. Then heat a griddle pan until it is very hot. Add some olive oil to the pan and then cook the halibut for around 2-3 minutes on each side. The griddle pan should leave black stripes across the flesh. Check it is cooked through to the middle before serving.

To serve

Place the crab crushed potatoes in the centre of a warmed plate. Place the halibut on top and spoon over the salsa. Heat the red pepper sauce and drizzle around the fish. Serve with cooked samphire.

Cream of the COTSWOLDS

With nearly a century of ice cream-making knowledge, Winstones Cotswold Ice Cream is a story that begins in a farmhouse kitchen with a family recipe...

The Winstones name is a familiar sight across the Cotswolds. The family-run business has been making ice cream since 1925 and today the products are on sale far and wide across restaurants, cafés, delis, local stores and farm shops, as well as from their own parlour and five ice cream vans, of course.

When it comes to serving ice cream on the move, Winstones are a family who have more than a little experience up their sleeves. The story began with Albert and Doris Winstone, the grandparents of current owner Jane. Albert began making ice cream from his home kitchen using a classic Victorian recipe when the business he worked for as a French polisher closed down. Selling his homemade ice cream on the neighbouring golf course soon earnt him a reputation locally – and before long, Winstones Ice Cream was born.

As the reputation for quality spread, the business grew, with the shed becoming a small kiosk and soon after a parlour. An interest in WW1 motorbikes inspired him to build a side-car and begin to take his ice creams to the local area. Today five vintage and modern ice cream vans continue this tradition!

Over the last 90 years the business has continued to expand, first under their son Frank and today their granddaughter Jane. Despite the demand for their produce, the family have remained true to the heritage of the business – the milk and cream are still sourced locally and they use seasonal British ingredients to inspire their flavour range. Think spiced plums in winter and rhubarb crumble in summer, alongside those classics like mint choc chip, vanilla or raspberry ripple.

The parlour is open all year round, serving hot Belgian waffles and delicious hot chocolates to those who would rather have something warm in the winter months. For most people, however, it's never too cold for a Winstones ice cream!

As the company grew rapidly, the family made a decision not to move towards stocking large supermarket chains and keep the focus firmly on their Gloucestershire base. By keeping production local, they find they have more control over choosing the very best ingredients, working with regional suppliers and keeping quality at its highest... the way things have been since 1925.

Winstones
COTSWOLD ICE CREAM
Made with farm fresh milk
Toffee Ripple
(Vanilla Flavoured Ice Cream with Toffee Flavoured Syrup)
1 Litre
CONTAINS NON MILK FAT
Winstones
COTSWOLD ICE CREAM
Winstones
COTSWOLD
ICE CREAM
OPEN
DOUBLE CONE £3·20
WAFFLE CONE £2·10
TUB £1·60/£3·20/£4·80
FLAKE
FUDGE
NUTS
Winstones
COTSWOLD ICE CREAM
Made with farm fresh
ORGANIC milk
1 LITRE
Salted Caramel
Rum & Raisin
Winstones
COTSWOLD ICE CREAM

Winstones
SUMMER FRUIT KNICKERBOCKER GLORY

Knickerbocker Glory is traditionally served in a tall slender glass and is thought to have originated in the UK in the 1930s. We've chosen this recipe because it harks back to a time when our company was in its infancy and this would have been a new and exciting way to serve our delicious ice cream.

Preparation time: 15 minutes | Cooking time: 15 minutes | Serves 4

Ingredients

For the fruit coulis:

300g assorted summer fruits, washed (we used strawberries and raspberries)

1 tbsp caster sugar

1 tbsp cornflour

For assembling:

Winstone's Ice Cream Strawberries & Cream

Winstone's Ice Cream Vanilla

150ml double or whipping cream

1 tsp caster sugar

200g fresh strawberries, washed and hulled (or other summer fruits)

200g fresh raspberries, washed (or other summer fruits)

Method

For the fruit coulis

Place the fruits in a saucepan over a low to medium heat and bring to a simmer. Continue to simmer for around 10 minutes or until the fruit begins to soften. Add the sugar and continue to simmer, stirring occasionally, until all the sugar has dissolved. Add the cornflour and mix until fully combined. Remove from the heat and then strain the mix through a fine sieve into a bowl to remove any seeds. Set aside to cool in the fridge. Once cooled you are ready to assemble your knickerbockers.

For assembling

About 10-15 minutes before assembling, remove your ice cream from the freezer to soften slightly. In the meantime prepare your cream. Add the sugar to the double or whipping cream and whip the cream until it forms soft peaks.

Prepare each Knickerbocker Glory in a tall glass. Line the glass with fruit coulis, turning the glass to coat it with coulis then fill the bottom with a handful of strawberries and raspberries. Follow this with a generous helping of coulis, then layered scoops of Winstone's Strawberries & Cream and Winstone's Vanilla ice cream. Top off with more fruit coulis, whipped cream and more fresh fruit.

Serve with a long sundae spoon.

Photo: Caron Badkin/Shutterstock.com

The DIRECTORY

These great businesses have supported the making of this book; please support and enjoy them.

Beard & Sabre
Unit 2B Norcote Workshops
Norcote
Cirencester GL7 5RH
Telephone: 0800 689 3406
Website: www.BeardandSabre.co.uk
Combining tradition with vision to lead the craft cider revolution, classic and avant-garde drinks crafted with 100% rack and cloth pressed apple.

Beau's Bakehouse
Unit 1 Tanhouse Farm
Frampton-on-Severn,
Gloucestershire GL2 7EH
Telephone: 01452 741189
Website: www.beausbakehouse.co.uk
Beau's Bakehouse is a small bakery based in Frampton-on-Severn making all natural cakes, slices and biscuits using the best local ingredients available.

The Bell at Selsley
Bell Lane
Selsley, Stroud
Gloucestershire GL5 5JY
Telephone: 01453 753801
Website: www.thebellinnselsley.com
Your friendly country pub with rooms, here to give you a true taste of the Cotswolds and all that it has to offer. Serving real ales, locally sourced food and seasonal game.

Bibury Trout Farm
Bibury
Cirencester
Gloucestershire GL7 5NL
Telephone: 01285 740215
Website: www.biburytroutfarm.co.uk
One of the oldest trout farms in the country, open to visitors, producing top quality Rainbow and Brown Trout for both the restocking and table markets.

The Bisley House
Middle Street
Stroud
Gloucestershire
GL5 1DZ
Telephone: 01453 751328
Website: www.bisleyhouse.co.uk
A hidden gem of Stroud, the Bisley House is a newly renovated pub restaurant with a flair for modern European cuisine and British seasonal produce.

The Canteen
Daysmill
Nailsworth
Stroud GL6 0DU
Telephone: 01453 836172
Website: www.facebook.com/TheCanteenNailsworth
A quirky little cafe in Nailsworth, hidden in a courtyard, a lovely atmosphere and shabby-chic design. Breakfast, lunch, cakes and evening parties.

The Chef's Dozen
Island House
Lower High Street
Chipping Campden
Gloucestershire GL55 6AL
Telephone: 01386 840598
Website: www.thechefsdozen.co.uk
The Chef's Dozen is proudly located in Chipping Campden, in the Cotswolds: the hills surrounding the town and the fantastic produce found within them virtually write our menu for us, with wild produce and game being a particular passion.

Cotswold Gold Ltd
East Lodge Farm
Stanton,
Broadway WR127NH
Telephone: 01386 584748
Website: www.cotswoldgold.co.uk
Cotswold Gold is an Extra Virgin Cold Pressed Rapeseed Oil grown, pressed and bottled on the family farm in the Cotswolds.

Cotswold Taste Ltd
6 Bridge Close
Lechlade
Gloucestershire GL7 3EZ
Telephone: 01367 253695
Website: www.cotswoldtaste.co.uk
Cotswold Taste is the quality marque and member-owned organisation for local food and drink produced to high standards in the Cotswolds.

The Cotswolds Distillery
Phillip's Field, Whichford Road
Stourton
Shipston-on-Stour CV36 5HG
Telephone: 01608 238533
Website: www.cotswoldsdistillery.com
The first full-scale distillery in the Cotswolds. Home of outstanding natural spirits including Cotswolds Whisky and Cotswolds Dry Gin.

Court Farm Shop
Stoke Road
Stoke Orchard
Cheltenham
Gloucestershire GL52 7RY
Telephone: 01242 678374
Website: www.courtfarmshop.co.uk
Court Farm Shop and Butchery is built upon a strong history of traditional family farming, providing a full range of home produced and local products as well as a fantastic traditional butchery service.

Firbosa Hereford Meat Boxes
Fir Farm Ltd
Rectory Farm, Lower Swell
Gloucestershire GL54 1LH
Telephone: 01451 832385
Website: www.firbosaherefords.co.uk
Mixed sustainable farming enterprise producing beef, pork, lamb and eggs on a grass fed system.

The Fire Station
St. James Square
Cheltenham GL50 3PU
Telephone: 01242 809135
Website:
www.thefirestationcheltenham.co.uk
A vibrant, fresh and accessible all-day social hub, The Fire Station provides a welcoming space that everyone feels they can use as they like, when they like, to eat, drink, work and party.

The Grape Escape Wine Bar & Merchant
10 Bath Road
Cheltenham GL53 7HA
Telephone: 01242 256716
Website: www.thecheltenhamgrape.com
Cheltenham wine bar with a weekly changing by-the-glass list and over 300 bottles to choose from.

Henry's Coffee House & Dairy
3-4 Market Square
Minchinhampton
Stroud GL6 9BW
Telephone: 01453 886855
Website: www.woefuldanedairy.co.uk
www.facebook.com/HenrysCoffeeDairy
Henry's, where handmade organic dairy produce and great vibes come hand in hand.

The Hog
The Cross
Horsley
Stroud GL6 0PR
Telephone: 01453 833843
Website: www.thehogathorsley.co.uk
The Hog at Horsley is a vibrant, family-run freehouse in the village of Horsley.

Huxleys
High Street
Chipping Campden
Gloucestershire GL55 6AL
Telephone: 01386 849077
Website: www.huxleys.org
Huxleys is a café and bar with an excellent wine list, coffee selection and antipasti menu.

Jesse Smith Butchers

Jesse Smith Farm Shop and Coffee Shop
Unit 13A, 19 Love Lane
Cirencester GL7 1YG
Telephone: 01285 653352

Jesse Smith Cirencester
Blackjack Street
Cirencester GL7 2AA
Telephone: 01285 653387

Jesse Smith Tetbury
Long Street
Tetbury GL8 8AA
Telephone: 01666 502730

W. J. Castle Burford
High Street
Burford, Oxon OX8 4RG
Telephone: 01993 822113

W. J. Castle Northleach
The Green, Northleach
Cheltenham GL54 3EX
Telephone: 01451 860243
Website: www.jessesmith.co.uk
Butchers with passion and pride. Established in the heart of the Cotswolds in 1808 built on the foundations of impeccable quality & exceptional service.

Kibousushi
18 Regent Street
Cheltenham
Gloucestershire GL50 1HE
Telephone: 01242 300161
Website: www.kibousushi.com
Award-winning Japanese kitchen, ramen and sushi bar in the heart of Cheltenham.

Lavender Bakehouse & Coffee Shop
20 London Road
Chalford
Stroud GL6 8NW
Telephone: 01453 889239
website: www.lavenderbakehouse.co.uk
Coffee shop bistro serving breakfast, lunch, afternoon tea, coffee and cake.

Le Champignon Sauvage
24-28 Suffolk Road
Cheltenham GL50 2AQ
Telephone: 01242 573449
Website:
www.lechampignonsauvage.co.uk
Situated within the historic spa town of Cheltenham, two Michelin star Le Champignon Sauvage is the perfect place to relax whilst visiting the Cotswolds.

The Little Pickle
Bourton-on-the-Water,
Gloucestershire
Telephone: 077483 89941 / 07966 724695
Website: www.thelittlepickle.co.uk
Bespoke catering company based in the Cotswolds offering catering for all kinds of events as well as pop-up dining and providing their own range of pickles and preserves.

Made by Bob
The Corn Hall
Unit 6 The Corn Hall
26 Market Place
Cirencester GL7 2NY
Telephone: 01285 641818
Website: www.foodmadebybob.com
A Michelin-recognised restaurant and deli in the centre of Cirencester with a daily changing menu.

Morris & Brown Café at Broadway Tower
Middle Hill
Broadway
Worcestershire WR12 7LB
Telephone: 01386 852945 (Morris & Brown cafe)
Website: www.broadwaytower.co.uk
Sharing a site with Broadway Tower, one of the country's finest viewpoints, our Morris & Brown cafe serves tasty and imaginative food throughout the day - choose between the cosy, contemporary-style interior or terrace al fresco dining, surrounded by stunning views.

No. 23 Bar & Bistro
23 Nelson Street
Stroud GL5 2HH
Telephone: 01453 298525
Website: www.no23stroud.com
No. 23 is an independent bistro in Stroud, created to celebrate the love of good food and good company.

The Old Stocks Inn
The Square
Stow-on-the-Wold
Gloucestershire GL54 1AF
Telephone: 01451 830666
Website: www.oldstocksinn.com
16th-century boutique inn, nestled in the heart of The Cotswolds.

The Ox
10 Cambray Place
Cheltenham GL50 1JS
Telephone: 01242 234779
Website: www.theoxcheltenham.com
The Ox is a bastion of simple, top notch, British fare, cooked to impeccable standards.

Prithvi
37 Bath Road
Cheltenham GL537HG
Telephone: 01242 226229
Website: www.prithvirestaurant.com
A refined and sophisticated approach to Indian dining in an intimate and relaxed surrounding.

Rave Coffee Limited
Unit 7 Stirling Works
Love Lane Industrial Estate
Cirencester
Gloucestershire GL7 1YG
Telephone: 01285 651884
Website: www.ravecoffee.co.uk
Speciality coffee roasters with an on-site café.

Relish Events
51 Castle Street
Cirencester GL7 1QD
Telephone: 01285 658 444
Website: www.relishevent.co.uk
Based in Cirencester's idyllic high street, we cater for high-end events and host weddings, private parties and corporate occasions, all tailored to our clients' needs.

StarBistro
National Star, Ullenwood
Cheltenham GL53 9QU
Telephone: 01242 535984

StarBistro
12 Royal Crescent
Cheltenham GL50 3DA
Telephone: 01242 572958
Website: www.starbistro.org
In addition to serving some of the finest food from the Cotswolds, both of our StarBistros offer young people with disabilities the opportunity to gain real work experience within a bustling hospitality environment.

The Straw Kitchen
Whichford Pottery
Whichford
Shipston on Stour CV36 5PG
Telephone: 01608 685950
Overlooking the rolling Cotswold hills and nestled between its bumpy straw bale walls, The Straw Kitchen offers a globally inspired seasonal menu, exquisite coffee and cakes to die for.

Stroud Brewery Ltd
Unit 11, Phoenix Works
Hope Mill Lane, Thrupp
Stroud GL5 2BU
Telephone: 01453 887122
Website: www.stroudbrewery.co.uk
At Stroud Brewery we have crafted a range of organic and vegan beers made with barley grown on the surrounding Cotswolds hills.

Stroud Farmers Market
Cornhill Market Square
(and surrounding streets)
Cornhill
Stroud GL5 2HH
Telephone: 01453 758060
Website: www.fresh-n-local.co.uk
Stroud Farmers Market every saturday 9-2pm. We organise farmers' markets in Stroud, Gloucester, Stow-on-the-Wold and Swindon.

The Sweet Potato Spirit Company Limited
Unit 4C Asparagus Way
Vale Park Business Centre
Evesham
Worcestershire WR11 1GD
Telephone: 01386 446648
Website:
www.thesweetpotatospiritcompany.com
Welcome to our world where our twin passions, sweet potatoes and artisan distilling, are mixed daily.

The Vault
Waterloo House
Nailsworth
Gloucestershire GL6 0AQ
Telephone: 01453 833666
Website: www.thevaultnailsworth.co.uk
Tapas bar and restaurant in Nailsworth – fusion kitchen, wine, cocktails.

The White Spoon
8 Well Walk
Cheltenham
Gloucestershire GL50 3JX
Telephone: 01242 228555
Website: www.thewhitespoon.co.uk
Based in the heart of the Cotswolds, The White Spoon celebrates seasonal produce, accompanied by a fantastic drinks selection in a relaxed atmosphere.

William's Food Hall & Oyster Bar
3 Fountain Street
Nailsworth GL6 0BL
Telephone: 01453 832240
Website: www.williamsfoodhall.co.uk
Award-winning delicatessen and oyster bar – one of Rick Stein's 'Food Heroes' and Matthew Fort's 'Five Favourite Places to Shop'.

Winstones Ice Cream Ltd
Greenacres
Bowham
Stroud GL5 5BX
Telephone: 01453 873270
Website:
www.winstonesicecream.co.uk
Artisan ice cream since 1925.

Other titles in the 'Get Stuck In' series

The North Yorkshire Cook Book features Andrew Pern, Visit York, Made in Malton, Black Sheep Brewery and lots more.
978-1-910863-12-1

The Birmingham Cook Book features Glynn Purnell, The Smoke Haus, Loaf Bakery, Simpsons and lots more.
978-1-910863-10-7

The Bristol Cook Book features Dean Edwards, Lido, Clifton Sausage, The Ox, and wines from Corks of Cotham plus lots more.
978-1-910863-14-5

The Oxfordshire Cook Book features Mike North of The Nut Tree Inn, Sudbury House, Jacobs Inn, The Muddy Duck and lots more.
978-1-910863-08-4

The Lancashire Cook Book features Andrew Nutter of Nutters Restaurant, Bertram's, The Blue Mallard and lots more.
978-1-910863-09-1

The Liverpool Cook Book features Burnt Truffle, The Art School, Fraiche, Villaggio Cucina and many more.
978-1-910863-15-2

The Sheffield Cook Book - Second Helpings features Jameson's Tea Rooms, Craft & Dough, The Wortley Arms, The Holt, Grind Café and lots more.
978-1-910863-16-9

The Leeds Cook Book features The Boxtree, Crafthouse, Stockdales of Yorkshire and lots more.
978-1-910863-18-3

The Cambridgeshire Cook Book features Daniel Clifford of Midsummer House, The Pint Shop, Gog Magog Hills, Clare College and lots more.
978-0-9928981-9-9

The Suffolk Cook Book features Jimmy Doherty of Jimmy's Farm, Gressingham Duck and lots more.
978-1-910863-02-2

The Manchester Cook Book features Aiden Byrne, Simon Rogan, Harvey Nichols and lots more.
978-1-910863-01-5

The Lincolnshire Cook Book features Colin McGurran of Winteringham Fields, TV chef Rachel Green, San Pietro and lots more.
978-1-910863-05-3

The Newcastle Cook Book features David Coulson of Peace & Loaf, Bealim House, Grainger Market, Quilliam Brothers and lots more.
978-1-910863-04-6

The Cheshire Cook Book features Simon Radley of The Chester Grosvenor, The Chef's Table, Great North Pie Co., Harthill Cookery School and lots more.
978-1-910863-07-7

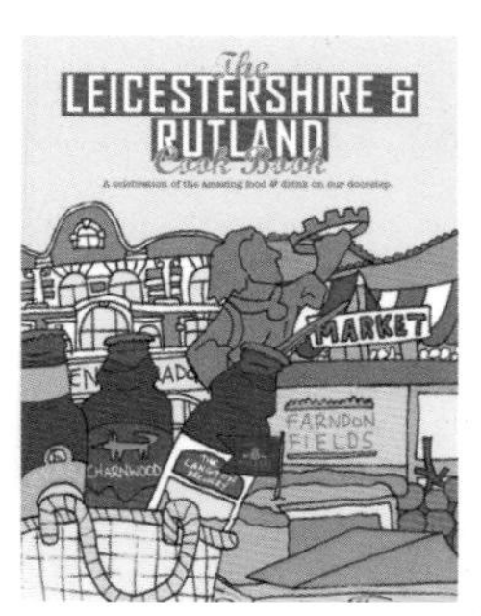

The Leicestershire & Rutland Cook Book features Tim Hart of Hambleton Hall, John's House, Farndon Fields, Leicester Market, Walter Smith and lots more.
978-0-9928981-8-2

All books in this series are available from Waterstones, Amazon and independent bookshops.

FIND OUT MORE ABOUT US AT WWW.MEZEPUBLISHING.CO.UK